CW01461002

Making Your Life A Christian Life

The Desert Fathers and St Francis of Assisi as Guides

by

Paul S. Russell

authorHOUSE®

AuthorHouse™
1663 Liberty Drive, Suite 200
Bloomington, IN 47403
www.authorhouse.com
Phone: 1-800-839-8640

First published by AuthorHouse 6/3/2009

ISBN: 978-1-4389-2338-3 (sc)

Library of Congress Control Number: 2009902197

*Printed in the United States of America
Bloomington, Indiana*

This book is printed on acid-free paper.

*I dedicate this book to my nephew,
William Russell McCurdy and all other men and
boys who suffer from Barth Syndrome.*

*Their courage and good cheer is a potent witness
to the strength of the human spirit, as is the
dauntlessness of those who love them.*

*All of them are proof that the fortitude of the
people we see in this book is still among us, today, if
we only know where to look.*

"A book should consist of examples."
--Ludwig Wittgenstein

Table of Contents

HOW TO USE THIS BOOK

This book is designed to offer you two things: an introduction to how Christian people have tried to dedicate their lives more fully to their faith in the past and some guidance in dedicating your own life more fully to following Christ in the future. I attempt to do the first of those things by offering you a brief overview of what is known of the very earliest Christians who tried to set their lives apart from the common pattern lived by those around them. We will consider what these early Christians found in Scripture to serve as guidelines for their own attempts, take a look at the very famous (but often misunderstood) desert dwelling Christians of ancient Egypt and then turn to the western stream of Christianity by looking at Francis of Assisi, in some ways an example of a person impelled by the same urge as those desert monks. ("Monk" can refer to either a man or woman; it means only someone who has dedicated himself to living alone without a family.) The final section of the book will try to sum up what we have seen, to draw some general lessons from these diverse sources and then to suggest some practical things for you to do if you decide to focus consciously on making your own life more Christian.

I make no claim to be a great example of Christian success. Luckily, it is not necessary that I should be a great saint myself in order to be able to teach you something about them. Christians have always recorded the lives and sayings of those they were convinced were good examples of conduct and teaching. *The Book of Acts* (6:8-7:60), in its narrative of the trial and death of Stephen contains what must be acknowledged as the earliest account of the martyrdom of a Christian (if we decide not to count Jesus as a Christian, which I think is best). This kind of writing is generally referred to as a "martyr **act**" because it records what the person **did** as a witness to his faith in Jesus Christ, a faith that led to his death. (The Greek word "martyr" means "witness".) Although Roman Catholic and Orthodox Christians have generally been more comfortable with the idea of reading and learning from saints' lives, the popularity of *Foxe's Book of Christian Martyrs* and the presence in any "Christian bookstore" of shelves of lives of faithful Christians (called "Christian Biography" to avoid the term "saints' lives", which sounds too "catholic") is clear proof that this approach to learning from the Christian past is alive and well in all branches of the Church. All Christians, whether great saints, themselves, or miserable sinners, can learn from reading these accounts of those whose sense of purpose and purity of dedication was greater than their own. We can hope that the contrast of what others have done with our feeble actions will spur us on to try to make our own lives a little bit less distant from these examples of fervor and holiness.

I suggest that, the first time you work your way through this book, you read the general introduction, which comes directly after this chapter, and then the two sets of chapters about the desert monks and the Poor Man of Assisi (a common way of referring to St. Francis). Then you should finish with the summary of what these chapters have contained. This will give you a sense of the history and character of these earlier Christians. The second time through, you should use the chapters on the Desert and Francis as spiritual reading. Each one has a prayer at its close (and most have one at the start). Set aside some time each day to read one of these chapters and pray the prayer at the close, asking God to help you glean all that may be useful for you from what you have read. There are 14 of these chapters, so this will take you two weeks. (It may be best if you skip the Sunday Sermons as you go by them on the Fridays and leave them for the Sunday of each week. They do not need to be read in their place in the sequence, though they would not mean much if they were read first, I think.) I have spent a number of years reading a sermon each day and have found it a very helpful discipline and, spiritually, most enriching. Two weeks may not be long enough for you to get a sense of what this practice can offer, but it will help you see different things in this material than just reading it for its information can. Both approaches to it are useful, but they are very different in intent and result.

If you are a member of a Bible Study group or reading group interested in taking on a religious book, you may want to read the book's introduction as background and then begin discussing the material with the chapters on the picture of religious life in the Scripture and the early Church. If you allow one meeting for that chapter, or two meetings to allow for fuller discussion (much, if not all, of that material is likely to be new to your members), you can then work through the sets of chapters on the Desert and Francis as complete wholes in just two meetings (if you are impatient or knowledgeable), you can take two of these chapters for each meeting (if you feel comfortable with what they contain) or take them one chapter at a time. (This last way is best, if you have the time and patience.)

Because this approach to learning about Dedicated Christian Life requires two things from you: that you have a grasp of what these early Christians actually did, as well a religious appreciation of why they did it and what they thought it meant, it makes good sense to think that you have not really taken in what it has to offer you if you only look at it once. I think this material is both interesting and inspiring. It gives me a sense of my own lukewarm character as a Christian (which is not a comforting thought in light of *Revelation* 3:14-16) and shows me a whole variety of ways in which I can turn that insufficient ardor into something worthy of a servant of God. I finish writing this book feeling its challenge very deeply. I hope that you feel this call to serious discipleship, too, and pray for me as I struggle to meet it. I will surely be praying for you.

INTRODUCTION

There has always been a desire among Christians to learn about their faith and how to live it by hearing and telling stories about their forbears in the Faith. The popularity of the little book of devotion commonly called *The Protevangelium of James*[1], which tells the story of what happened *before* the New Testament gospels pick up the story (the infancy of the Virgin Mary, etc) and of the allegorical novel by John Bunyan, *The Pilgrim's Progress* shows evidence of this same desire. Some of this, of course, comes from the simple pleasures of hearing entertaining stories, but there is also evidence here of a sense that stories work better than essays at communicating the elements of religious life. (I am trained in the History of Christian Doctrine, and so am better equipped than most, I suppose, to read treatises on Christian Thought, but I feel this preference for stories as much as anyone. It is a natural human urge, I think.) Christian life is a subject that is very well suited to being discussed and taught in this way.

Christian life is a mix of trying to reach the same goal as everyone else: sanctity and closeness to God, and trying to do so in your own life in your own place and

---

[1] The standard English translation of this can be found at 370-388 in Edger Hennecke, *New Testament Apopcrypha* (edited by Wiiliam Schneemelcher) Volume One Gospels and Related Writings Philadelphia: The Westminster Press 1963. It can also be found in a variety of recently published collections of early Christian material. Many public libraries and popular bookstores now contain copies of one or more of these.

time. No Christian should want to be different from all other Christians just to be different, but each of us must find his own, possibly unique, way to be a fully Christian version of himself.

Not only must we allow for the potential for individuality in religious life, but we should also expect that our approach will change in its details as our life goes on. Even if I had been a perfect saint at age 15 (I wasn't) I would not still have been perfect if I had been unchanged as a married adult of 28. Now, after 20 years of marriage and the birth of three children, my life must, if it is to be even a rough approximation of what it ought to be, have changed very radically again. I expect that this pattern will hold true for the rest of the days God grants me to live on earth. How could it not be so? It is virtuous to yell "Fire" if one is breaking out in a building where you are, but not otherwise.[2] What actions are right changes as our circumstances change. This means important things for how you should read this book and what you should expect from it.

The topic of how to live a Christian religious life must be approached with an open mind. Of course, you must use your best judgment and your knowledge of Christianity and of life in general, but you must not expect to find stories about Christians who are just like you or just like people you know. We will be looking at, and thinking about, people who lived in far distant places a long time ago. The cultures they knew, the places they visited, the people they saw and the lives they led were all very different from our modern western experiences. This does not

---

[2] See *Ecclesiastes* 3:1-8

mean that they were any less Christian than we are (or can be); it only means that their attempts to live as Christians were formed to fit into a very different framework than ours must be. This means that we must be "wise as serpents, and harmless as doves"[3] if we are to learn from them. We must be harmless doves where we allow their words and actions to approach (and reproach) us if they show us areas in which our understanding has been faulty and our fervor has been cool. We must also, however, be as wise as serpents when we are translating the particularities of their lives into principles that can apply to us and, what is also very important, when we recognize the short-comings that they also suffered from. Every age has its blind spots and every person has his limitations, both avoidable and unavoidable. We should not expect to find perfection in any human being (except Jesus, but He is the exception in this, as He is in so much else). This does not mean that we cannot learn from others and it does not mean that the time we spend on considering others' lives as examples is wasted. It merely means that we must use our brains as well as our eyes and ears if we are to live as fully-engaged Christians.

So, you have been warned! I will do my honest best to tell you about things that I think will help you understand more clearly what Christian faith should mean to us and how it can be expressed in actual daily living. You, on the other hand, must be willing to listen to what I have to say, to look at what I try to show you and to reflect honestly on what it offers and how you can best benefit from your contact with it. I never come away from

---

[3] *Matthew* 10:16

thinking about these things without the conviction that I have profited greatly. Of course, my application of what I learn is not perfect and I continue to need to return to these examples to be challenged again. I hope that you will find this volume as helpful as I have (and that you will make better use of it than I have). There is much that other Christians can do to help us, if we give them the chance to do so. If you agree with that sentiment after reading what follows, I will think that my effort has not been wasted.

[Note: this book contains many quotations from earlier work and from original sources. When I have written and attached a note of explanation to one of these passages, I have ended it with the notation: "(author's note)", just to make certain that you can tell which words are mine and which are the ones I am quoting. Any other notes are part of the text I am citing.

Because I am a member of a Christian communion that uses the *King James Version* of the Bible in its worship, and because I think that version is still the most familiar one among English speaking people, I have chosen to use it whenever I am quoting Scripture.]

THE EARLY BACKGROUND

Before we move on to look at our central examples of dedicated Christian life, St. Francis of Assisi and the Desert Fathers, we should consider the broader history of this element in Christianity of people devoting themselves to trying to live their Christian faith as fully as possible. This will allow us to develop some sense of the background that lies behind the two examples we will examine more closely.

The idea that there are some among the faithful who would like to pour themselves into their religious life more intently than their fellows is not something that was invented out of nowhere by these more intense believers. This sense of a special calling to religious living is not an invention of the later Church. Scripture shows us people who were especially dedicated to God, both in the sense of being set apart for His service from an early age (Samuel, Samson, John the Baptist) as well as those who were called later in life to do His will in the world (Moses, Isaiah, Jeremiah, Hosea).

Since we are in search of models from whom we can learn how to serve God better, it makes sense to set aside those called before their births (as, for example, John the Baptist) or those who were called by God against their will (for example, Jonah). The former group we cannot join, if we do not already belong to it, and the latter group we can hope to avoid by not resisting God's call when it comes to us in the future. Those who try to do what they think they are called to do are those who are swimming in the same stream that we are, so it is to them that we should turn for guidance and fellowship.

The biblical record and the history of the Church show that there have always been those who were particularly determined to make progress in their religious lives. It is not often that we are told much about what they **did** as a result of this desire, but there are some hints available to us, if we are willing to look for them.

John the Baptist is an example of one who lived a life designed to make him ready and worthy for the task ahead, which, for him, was proclaiming the advent of the Messiah. His unique role in the history of God's work in the world makes him an unlikely candidate for being someone we can imitate very closely. The Messiah has already come and our task is to live in the light of that completed revelation. The details of John's life apart from his connection to Jesus are almost completely unknown to us. The gospels tell us only about the most individual and, so, the most unrepresentative, aspects of his life. There is almost nothing we know about him that seems applicable to the general Christian life. (This same fact sets all the Old Testament prophets off as difficult examples for us to follow. Their individual calls seem imbedded in a different age than the one we know.) We will do better, then, to set him aside as a possible source of help. The obvious place for finding models of life is among the number of Christians who lived after our Lord's Resurrection, because they lived in the theological world that we know: in the light of the whole of Jesus' earthly life and as a part of the Church militant, struggling here in the world.

Once the Roman state had noticed the early Church and had classified it as a menace to public order, early Christian were dedicating themselves to their faith in very real ways every time they ventured out to attend a service of worship. Anyone willing to persevere in participating in the life of the Church during the time of the persecutions was involved at a very high risk. The periodic outbreaks of persecutions in the early centuries would repeatedly purge the Church of its uncommitted members and furnish new examples of those willing to suffer for their faith.

Any Christian forced to suffer for his faith could be a confessor or martyr.[4] This is an important point to keep in mind as we look at this early period.

The early Church was a worshipping and evangelistic body. It contained those trying to live Christian lives and was a support to them in hard times:

- In financial hard times, it would try to support its members through practical charity.

- In times of persecution, it would support its members morally and spiritually, through prayers and visiting. (Visiting those who had been cast into prison, something that we see already in the case of St. Paul[5], continues through the ancient

---

[4] In later Christian terms, a "confessor" was someone who had suffered for his faith, through imprisonment or torture, for example, while a "martyr" was someone who had "witnessed" (the Greek word "martyr" means "witness") to his faith by giving up his life rather than abandon it.

[5] The very last scene in *Acts*, 28:30-31, describes St. Paul receiving visitors just outside the bounds of the city of Rome and continuing to teach them about the Christian Way. This mix of oppression with freedom (arresting Paul but allowing him to keep doing what he had been arrested for) is very hard for modern readers to imagine, since they are used to modern totalitarian governments and their more ruthless and consistent approach to the persecution of those they consider dangerous.

period. It seems very odd to us that the Roman authorities would allow Christians to visit their fellows who were in prison for being Christians and not arrest the visitors, but there is no doubt that it happened.)

It is clear that all the experiences that went along with the onset of persecutions [the anticipatory worry, the temptation to forsake the Church, the worshipping while under threat of arrest, the caring for the families of those in prison, the visiting of the prisoners, the attendance at their trials (and executions), the care of their bodies and the subsequent memorials on the anniversaries of their deaths] were all formative elements in the growing awareness of Christians of themselves as a group set apart from those around them. The cost of discipleship[6] and the brotherhood of those willing to pay that cost were firmly imprinted on the Christian mind in the first 300 years of Christianity. The Church could not remember ever having lived without the strain and inspiration of this aggression. What would take their place after 324 AD, when Constantine declared the religion legal throughout the Roman Empire? Would they leave only a void behind?

Three centuries of holding martyrs up as the model of devotion, beginning with Stephen in *Acts* 7, meant that 12 generations of Christians had been accustomed to thinking along these lines. It should not be surprising that those who followed after them felt impelled to find

---

[6] To use the title of the famous book by a modern martyr, Dietrich Bonhoeffer.

a way to pursue their faith with the same fervor that they had thought of as the mark of the Church up to then.

It would be a mistake, however, to think that ascetical Christian life was created as a replacement for martyrdom without its having held any previous place in the Christian imagination. Things in history are seldom so simple. As a matter of fact, it can be demonstrated that martyrdom, in some areas, came into the Church when a sophisticated system of ascetical practices already existed there.[7] It makes the most sense to think of a situation in which the growing desire to live more serious Christian lives was bolstered by the disappearance of martyrdom as a possibility for doing so. The combination of these two circumstances could easily have supported an interest in serious devotion to religious advancement among Christians.[8]

The gospels contain startling and challenging calls by Jesus to complete selfless devotion to Him on the part of His followers. Two of them leap to my mind as I write:

> Whosoever therefore shall confess me
> before men, him will I confess also
> before my Father which is in heaven.
> But whosoever shall deny me before
> men, him will I also deny before my
> Father which is in heaven.
> Think not that I am come to send peace

---

[7] Harvey mentions this at 100-101.
[8] Brock, Asceticism, 2-3, mentions both the connection with martyrdom and the fact of the previous existence of the ascetical impulse in the Syrian Church.

on earth: I came not to send peace, but a sword.

For I am come to set a man at variance against his father, and the daughter against her mother, and the daughter in law against her mother in law.

And a man's foes shall be they of his own household.

He that loveth father or mother more than me is not worthy of me: and he that loveth son or daughter more than me is not worthy of me.

And he that taketh not his cross, and followeth after me, is not worthy of me.

He that findeth his life shall lose it: and he that loseth his life for my sake shall find it.

(Matthew 10:32-39)

And he said to them all, If any man will come after me, let him deny himself, and take up his cross daily, and follow me.

For whosoever will save his life shall lose it: but whosoever will lose his life for my sake, the same shall save it.

For what is a man advantaged, if he gain the whole world, and lose himself, or be cast away?

For whosoever shall be ashamed of me and of my words, of him shall the Son

of man be ashamed, when he shall come
in his own glory, and in his Father's, and
of the holy angels.
               (*Luke* 9:23-26)

There is no need to multiply these citations when
they are so well known. The urge to follow Jesus exclu-
sively while giving no thought to anything else is one that
many Christians have felt in their lives. Some ages are
more prone to taking the Lord's words at their face value
than others, but all ages have produced people who have
felt that urge strongly enough to act on it. Making note
of this element in Jesus' teaching is important because it,
again, makes clear that an energetic approach to Christian living is not out of place in the Church but, instead,
is a natural response to a challenge that was present in the
Gospel from the life of Jesus onwards. (In our lukewarm
age, this reminder is necessary while, in other, more
strenuous times, it might have been necessary to make
the point that not every Christian need follow Our Lord
in precisely the same way, especially in the most demanding, counter-cultural way. Each age has its own characteristic tendencies and each has its own blind spots.)

With that sketch of general points in mind, let us go
back to the beginning of this process and embark on a
more fully fleshed-out over-view of this early strain of
dedicated religious life as it is seen in the Bible and the
early Church. Our goal will be to gain a rounded sense of
what the people of God throughout this long period tried
to do if they felt an urge to apply themselves more strenu-
ously to religious living than the majority of their fellows
did. We will hope that their insight and actions will help
us put our two central examples more clearly in focus and
also provide us with food for our own reflections, at the
end of this volume and after we have set it aside.

Chapter 1

STUDYING CHRISTIAN LIFE IN SCRIPTURE AND THE EARLY CHURCH

There is a natural tendency in human beings to dwell on extreme examples when they discuss things. This makes perfect sense:

- Extreme examples make one's point very clearly.
- There is a lot of information about extreme cases for people to use (because they excite so much notice).
- Extreme cases make good stories.

Still, it is important to realize that extreme examples are not necessarily all the cases of a certain kind that exist or the most useful if one is searching for guidance and encouragement.

The Church has made much of martyrdom, of striking ascetics like the Desert Fathers and of charismatic individuals like Francis of Assisi. This does not mean, however, that only people of an unusual sort can hope to live out a full Christian calling. It is important to be aware that we can see evidence of less unusual people having great success at being faithful all through the long age that marked the period described by the Bible and the early age of the Church. In fact, it is worth beginning our over-view with these people in mind.

Scripture shows many examples of people who had a special sense of their dedication to the service of God: famous cases are Jeremiah and Moses. However, Scripture also shows a pattern for virtue that is not set aside as the province of the specially gifted or the specially chosen. Obvious examples can be found in Psalms 1 and 15, both of which describe the profile of a righteous man. [The Bible certainly does not deny that women can be righteous (indeed *Proverbs* 31 is famous for its description of one kind of righteous life a woman might lead) but there is no doubt that the usual way of discussing virtue in Scripture is by describing a righteous man. The Holy Spirit trusts that we are able to abstract the principles put forward in these passages and that, if we do, we will find that they apply equally well to both male and female believers.] We will use these principles later to help us pick out the general characteristics of the faithful human being.

An examination of the early history of the Church also shows examples of many different kinds of holiness.

The harsh treatment that many Christians faced and the fervor necessary for anyone to leave family, friends and history behind to embrace a new religious life and new community of faith, largely made up of strangers, meant that the whole tenor of Christian life in the early generations was pitched in a higher key than our more sedate Christian lives usually know. This would naturally tend to attract the Christians of that time even more to examples of extreme hardships undergone and of outstanding fervor and devotion. The pressure to apostasize and forswear the allegiance to Christ that the Church felt as a part of its inheritance meant that those who resisted that pressure most completely (martyrs) held a special place in the Church's heart.

Still, the Church always had a clear idea of holiness that did not include or require martyrdom. The earliest surviving Christian treatise on prayer, by the great scholar Origen, of Alexandria in Egypt, will show us this clearly when we examine it. We will also look at the *Letter to Marcellinus* of Athanasius of Alexandria, the earliest discussion of the use of the Psalms in prayer and devotion. Together, these two works will bring us into contact with early Christian voices on prayer and the use of the Bible in our religious lives. These works address Christian life of the sort that most of us lead.

Along these same lines, it is important for us to be aware that the most consistently rigorous region that we know of in the early Church, the Syriac[9] speaking Middle East, did not think that the only examples worth follow-

---

[9] Syriac is a dialect of Aramaic that has been used most frequently by Christians. It is very closely connected, both linguistically and geographically, to Aramaic, which was the language of the early Jewish rabbis and, likely, the language Jesus spoke most commonly. There is some scholarly debate as to whether the two are "really" separate languages at all. (That kind of question quickly goes beyond the grasp of anyone who is not a professional scholar of linguistics, and seems beside the point for the study of early Christianity and Judaism, anyway.) The main area of Syriac usage stretched from the eastern shore of the Mediterranean Sea to the western regions of Persia beyond Mesopotamia. Groups of Christians who speak a form of Syriac and use classical Syriac in their worship still survive in parts of the Middle East and in exile in the West. There is also a community of Christians in the state of Kerala in southern India who have used Syriac for their liturgical language as far back as they can be traced in history, which is at least to the Fourth Century AD.

ing were extreme ones that would keep a person from leading a normal life in touch with the larger society around him. The "Sons and Daughters of the Covenant", an order of life that existed only in the Syriac Church, will serve as our third element of early Christian living that has connections with, and resonance for, Christians of our own day who long to live their faith more fully and successfully.

The religious background against which the Desert Fathers began their lives in the desert and Francis heard the call to rebuild Christ's Church was one that knew and valued the extreme as well as the moderate, the unnoticed faithful believer as well as the strikingly idiosyncratic one. Everyone who meets or speaks about these people takes them to be outside the ordinary, but they are not so unusual that what they are trying to do is mysterious. Although they are special cases, the other Christian people who lived at the time of the flowering of the Egyptian Desert Tradition and during the life of Francis thought of them as being people who were trying to live out the same Christian faith that they were, only in a more intense and picturesque manner. That striking character makes them useful objects of study, even for us.

In the manner of the Christian imagination of the past, we will take our central examples from the realm of the exotic (they do, after all, provide much food for thought and many good stories) but we will do so with the intention of using those oddities as guides to constructing a more ordinary outline of how the Christian life may be lived. If we do our work well, we will come, in the end, to a picture of a dedicated Christian as someone who attempts to transform the life he has, rather than seeking to exchange it for an entirely new one. Because

I have no desire to leave my family as a part of following Jesus, I will hope to find a way for a Christian to transform and evangelize the world from within it, rather than as an outsider, looking in. If you are interested in the same search, you may find this process helpful, as I have. With that purpose in mind, we can now turn to look at a selected outline of the history of serious Christian living. This outline will help us appreciate the two extended examples we will look at afterwards.

Chapter 2

PSALMS 1 AND 15

If we are trying to get an idea of what the Scripture teaches about a religious life, we must do one of two things:

- We can carefully work through the whole Bible with religious life in mind and compile and synthesize all the relevant material we find in order to come to a responsible conclusion. (In the abstract, this approach would certainly be the best.)
- We can try to find a briefer part of the whole that is representative and easier to use.

Because time is pressing (the book does not need a 300 page section on the scriptural background of ideas on living religious lives) and I want to make progress in our task (and because I am not professionally trained in the academic study of Scripture and would be embarrassed to presume to undertake such a gargantuan task, or, at least, to do so in public) it seems best to be selective.

Where should we turn to find the Bible's idea of religious living expressed in a brief compass? What part of the Bible could possibly offer a better way into the mind and heart of the scriptural view of religious life than the Psalms, which were sung and recited by Jews and Christians in their public worship and private devotion all during the period of the gathering of the biblical books and still are used this way in our own day? Surely the words of the Psalms must have rung in the ears of believers as they tried to plan their lives and guide their own actions.

I have chosen to look at Psalms 1 and 15 from the 150 psalms available for us to use for these reasons: they are brief, they are directed at our topic of interest and their prominence in the biblical imagination argues that they express central ideas.[10] So, in the conviction that in choosing these two brief pieces we are making an intelligent, honest attempt to see what the Bible teaches (in its basic outlines) about the life of the religious person, we will turn to Psalms 1 and 15.

We will take three elements of each of these two psalms as special points of attention: its general tone, the details of its teaching and what the Psalm puts forward as the goal its teaching makes possible. The Psalms are bottomless wells we can never hope to empty, and time and space constraints (and the limits of my own abilities and insight) will force us to settle for just these three aspects in our reading, but they are reasonable keys to examine because they will help us to get a grasp of the psalms' general thrust.

Psalm 1

Blessed is the man that walketh not in the counsel of the

---

[10] After writing this chapter, I was reading *Jeremiah* and came upon echoes of Psalm 1 at *Jeremiah* 17:5-8. This example of its active presence in the minds of the faithful (for God is using its known imagery to give His point more force) is a good example of how these religious songs have always exercised their influence on God's people.

ungodly, nor standeth in the way of sinners, nor sitteth in the seat of the scornful.
But his delight is in the law of the LORD; and in his law doth he meditate day and night.
And he shall be like a tree planted by the rivers of water, that bringeth forth his fruit in his season; his leaf also shall not wither; and whatsoever he doeth shall prosper.
The ungodly are not so: but are like the chaff which the wind driveth away.
Therefore the ungodly shall not stand in the judgment, nor sinners in the congregation of the righteous.
For the LORD knoweth the way of the righteous: but the way of the ungodly shall perish.

The tone of this psalm is calm. There is no uncertainty and certainly no confusion. The man who is blessed is one who does not associate himself with those who do wrong. He does what is natural (according to his true nature) and in tune with creation and its Creator, so he is like a tree, maturing and growing as it should. Nature works against the ungodly: blowing them away in the wind like chaff, while it supports the blessed man in his life and work. "Whatsoever he doeth shall prosper."

The details that are discussed show the blessed man keeping himself away from others who have chosen the ungodly way. There is a negative aspect to the walk of the blessed man just as there is a positive one. The evil are taking counsel together (presumably for evil purposes). They seem to be organized in an attempt to further their schemes. The righteous also have a congregation and "stand in judgment", that is, they can survive the test of judgment without falling. Righteous people's lives have prepared them for that test. Human beings must be judging according to the law of the Lord and, since the blessed man meditates in it "day and night", his whole life works to prepare him to meet that judgment with confidence.

The result of this life, lived in the presence of the law of the Lord and separated from the scornful, ungodly and sinners, is that, as we saw before, the righteous man is blessed by God and helped by Him to become what God had intended him to be. He prospers in his work and finds himself to be fruitful and long-living. The psalm's words "his leaf also shall not wither" show that a full, natural life is the appropriate lot of the blessed man, for he is the man at one with himself and with the God Who created him.

This psalm does not present the life of the blessed as something that only the few and very exceptional can hope to achieve. Instead, that life is described through drawing clear pictures of the groups of people and kinds of activities to which the man attaches himself (or from which he detaches himself). The fact that all these things occur in groups shows that neither the righteous nor the ungodly can claim to be a rarity. This picture is one of a life of blessing worked out and lived within the human community. It is a blessed life that leads to the man being what God had intended him to be: taking his rightful place in this world and prospering in it. In the dry Middle East, it is the tree by the rivers of water that is where it would like to be and that is the kind of tree the blessed man is. He is in the place that God made him to occupy and he lives long and prosperously in it. This psalm, which serves as an introduction to the whole Psalter, depicts a kind of righteousness and blessing that enjoy the good things of this life, as well as receiving the approval of the Lord and a vivifying connection to Him through His law.

Psalm 15

Lord, who shall abide in thy tabernacle? who shall dwell in thy holy hill?
He that walketh uprightly, and worketh righteousness,
And speaketh the truth in his heart.
He that backbiteth not with his tongue, nor doeth evil to his neighbor, nor taketh up a reproach against his neighbor.
In whose eyes a vile person is contemned; but he honoreth them that fear the LORD.
He that sweareth to his own hurt, and changeth not.
He that putteth not out his money to usury, nor taketh reward against the innocent.
He that doeth these things shall never be moved.

This psalm begins with its focus more closely fixed on religious life than the first one did. "Abid[ing] in thy tabernacle" and "Dwell[ing] in thy holy hill" are both images of closeness to God in the context of worship. The "holy hill" is very likely meant to recall to our minds that Temple of the Lord on the hill in Jerusalem.[11] The

---

[11] This hill is traditionally identified with the Mount Moriah on which Abraham was intending to sacrifice Isaac when stopped by the angel of the Lord (see *Genesis* 22). (*The New Jerome Biblical Commentary* sec. 73:93, 1192) We cannot know whether this hill really was the same as that of Abraham's test, but the tradition does show how conscious the Jews were of the Temple's location on a hill-top.

tone is one of conviction and determination. The imaginative reader or singer of this psalm can feel the psalmist's teeth clench as he sets himself to the task of holding true to the place that he yearns to occupy. The psalm opens with the idea of "abiding", of staying and living in one settled place, and ends with "never be moved", showing that holding fast to what is right and not being distracted or drawn away from it will leave the true servant of the Lord in His presence. Faithful allegiance and connection to God are described in terms of proximity, and the one who does what he should is fixed, immovably, in the place he would like to be: in God's tabernacle.

The details are focused more on our relations with other people than in Psalm 1, though both imagine religious life being lived in a community. "Walk[ing] uprightly and work[ing] righteousness" are defined as "speaking the truth in [one's] heart", not "doing evil" or "backbiting" or "taking up a reproach" against one's neighbor. (This should remind us that loving our neighbor is an Old Testament teaching that Jesus picks up, supports and broadens by including all human beings in the "neighbor" category, not a new idea of His that was unknown before.[12]) Not putting one's money out to usury and not taking reward against the innocent are both ways of refusing to benefit unjustly from the misfortunes of others. It means not taking financial advantage of their need or helping to cheat those who are innocent but vulnerable to fraudulent attacks (presumably in court, where false

[12] See *Leviticus* 19:18. This comes in the middle of a chapter that would well repay the time to read it while thinking about the question of what kind of behavior the Old Testament teaches is righteous.

testimony could be offered for money). This upright person sticks to what is right even if it is not to his advantage ("He that sweareth to his own hurt, and changeth not.")

The one who does all these things will be fixed immovably in God's temple and on His holy hill. His closeness to God will never be put at risk. His behavior is such that he will not need to fear losing the religious benefits he has. They are a part of who and what he is and can never be changed or taken away, precisely because of the sort of person he is. His righteous actions define him and locate him.

How do these two psalms fit together to show a unified picture of the successful life of faith as the Old Testament presents it? A few obvious reflections will have to suffice for now. The blessing that God bestows on the righteous is both one of closeness to Him and of a chance to be what they should be in the world. The experience of believers and my own knowledge of the world do not make me think that everyone who does what he should will live a long and happy life on earth, but I do believe that he will benefit from his goodness because his life will be lived out in the context of a fulfilled connection with God and a religious closeness with Him. The clear focus on spiritual closeness to God as the reward of a righteous life in Psalm 15 is a useful balance to the picture in Psalm 1, which, taken on its own, might lead the unwary to think that stress-free lives come as a matter of course to those who are right with God. While Psalm 1 might leave the unwary reader with the idea that he can expect all his life to be spent by the rivers of water with his fruit never failing, Psalm 15 can serve to focus his gaze on the fact that the real reward of a religious life is *religious* and that we should not be shocked by trouble on the practical level.

Both of these psalms show the righteous man being righteous through his choice of those with whom he associates and how he acts in those associations. He stays away from the places where the wicked gather and keeps himself in the company of those doing right. He keeps himself acting appropriately in that company through his meditation on the Lord's law, which guides him in his actions, and in the judgments he offers when the righteous congregate. The righteous man of Psalm 15 is steadfast in his choices and, so, in his life. He "shall never be moved" because he continues to choose the right thing and, so, will not slide away. The success of the blessed man of Psalm 1 comes from his closeness to God and leads to his being close to God. This worldly success and the religious faithfulness he evinces are both parts of the same reality. This is the picture of a life that anyone willing to apply himself to it could lead.

It is difficult to know how the Jews of the Old Testament period, or even the members of the Church during the life of Jesus, lived their religion. Most of our sources are later and they do not contain the sort of reflection of the normal day to day practice of religion that we would like to have for this purpose. While the broad lines of the usual religious life of a pious Israelite can be pieced together from elsewhere in the Old Testament, the details of their activities are not known to us. This is where the Psalms come to the fore.

Psalms, because they served as a hymnal for religious services and as a book of prayers for private meditation, are perhaps the best place to turn for a window into the religious hearts of ancient Jews and Christians. Anyone attending synagogue worship, or even worship in the Temple in Jerusalem, would hear the Psalms as a central element in the services. By repetition, their words and tone would sink into the minds and hearts of the believers and become part of their religious bedrock. The things we saw in Psalms 1 and 15 above, through this life-long repetition, would have rung in the ears and replayed themselves in the thoughts of ancient Jews, God-fearers[13] and Christians who used them in their services. We can be quite confident that the picture we saw in these two psalms would have been known by all those who participated in scripturally-based worship. It is right for us to establish it in the background of our treatment of those involved in focused religious life later in the Christian tradition.

---

[13] This is the term commonly used in the ancient world for Gentiles who were well-disposed toward Judaism, read the Scriptures and tried to live moral lives according to the tenets of Jewish teaching but who stopped short of keeping the dietary laws and of undergoing formal conversion. These 'god-fearers' often attended synagogue worship and could be respected figures in the local Jewish community. Examples of these people can be found in the New Testament at *Luke* 7:1-10 and *Acts* 10:1-48. It is not surprising that Luke, the gentile evangelist, is interested in recording memories of these early gentile followers of Jesus.

Chapter 3

ORIGEN, ON PRAYER

Origen's (ca. 185-254) work, *On Prayer*, the earliest surviving Christian treatise on the subject, is useful both for its antiquity (it speaks from a time before both of our main subjects of study) and for the fact that it discusses the part of religious life that believers do on their own.[14] Since the worship of each local church would have been organized on a recognized standard pattern and could not be changed to follow the whims of individual believers (though we should imagine that this pattern might vary quite widely in detail from place to place) a member of a congregation in the early Church who wished to ratchet his religious practice up a notch or two would naturally do so in this more private realm. This is my reason for choosing this work as a source we should consider. Even the fact of its existence is witness to the presence of the idea that the individual believer could control his religious life in the small scale to suit his own ideas of propriety and effectiveness. (What would be the point of discussing prayer if Christians were not free to try to vary and improve their prayer lives?)

Where does Origen start in his examination of prayer? For him, prayer is not only a necessary part of the Christian life, it could be said that it is a place in which the Christian life expresses its identity. Origen's descrip-

---

[14] The easiest English version to find is in Greer, Origen. Oulton and Chadwick, Alexandrian Christianity, 238-329, also contains a very good translation with notes and an introduction. Both of these versions are available in paperback editions. All citations will refer to Greer's translation.

Paul S. Russell

tion of what preparation is necessary before we can even begin to pray is thus a fair place to find his ideas of what the Christian life is, at its most elemental.[15]

> The person praying must stretch out "holy hands" by thoroughly purging the passion of "anger" from his soul and harboring no rage against anyone and by forgiving each the sins he has committed against him (cf. 1 Tim. 2:8; Mt 6:12, 14; Lk 11:4). Next, so that his mind may not be muddied by thoughts from outside, he must forget for the time being everything but the prayer he is praying. (How can such a man fail to be highly blessed?)

Origen clearly does not think that the worship or ritual side of Christianity can exist in isolation from the rest of our lives. The pursuit of Christian living must be constant, not limited to the set times of corporate worship. The Christian life is a seamless whole for him. It includes the daily actions of life as well as the things that we customarily associate with worship.[16]

> And he prays "constantly" (deeds of virtue or fulfilling the commandments are included as part of prayer) who unites prayer with the deeds required and right deeds with prayer. For the only way we can accept the command to "pray constantly" (1 Thess. 5:17) as

---

[15] sec. IX.1, 98. (All the scripture references in these citations are a part of the published English version.)
[16] sec. XII.2, 104

32

referring to a real possibility is by saying that the entire life of the saint taken as a whole is a single great prayer. What is customarily called prayer is, then, a part of this prayer. Now prayer in the ordinary sense ought to be made no less than three times each day.

We see that Origen supposes (and commands) a planned regularity in the Christian life. Prayer must be woven into it in an intelligent, self-conscious way. (Note, also, that Scripture is the warrant and model for this position of his. Just after the quotation given above, Origen refers to Daniel's prayer, as mentioned in *Daniel* 6:13, as well as Peter's prayer in *Acts* 10 as setting out the ideal practice of a cycle of daily prayer.)

The Christian life is not a means of improving our earthly lot, in Origen's understanding, though God naturally[17] has a care for that element in our lives and includes it in His response to our prayers. (Origen's allowance for temporal blessings keeps him within reasonable distance of the picture we saw in Psalms 1 and 15, though his emphasis is clearly different.) This idea that the spiritual things in life and the spiritual gifts of God are greater than the material ones is not an unusual teaching in the history of the life of the

---

[17] I mean that literally: it is an attribute of God's nature that He should act this way.

Church. It allows for the connection and coexistence of the two emphases of the psalms we read while giving the preference to the religious or spiritual aspect, as one would expect.[18]

> You who wish to be spiritual, seek through your prayers heavenly and great things, so that in getting them as heavenly you may inherit the kingdom of heaven and in getting them as great you may enjoy good things. And as for the earthly and little things you need for your bodily necessities, the Father will supply you with them in proportion as you need them.

This seems to establish the broad outline of what our requests in prayer should be and allows petitionary prayer to include all the aspects of our lives in this world.

But there is more to prayer than just asking for things, as all Christians would agree. A description of prayer that

---

[18] Sec. XIV.1, 109. It is a point of historical interest, though not one of theological importance, that Origen preserves a saying from the Church's oral tradition about Jesus that runs along these lines. Greer, note 20, 83 says of this saying of Christ, which Origen gives on that page as "Seek the great things and the little things will be added for you; seek the heavenly things and the earthly things will be added for you.": "An agraphon or extracanonical saying (or sayings) of Christ. Cf. Jn. 3:12; Mt. 6:33; Lk. 12:31." He follows this with reference to some other early Christian authors who also record similar sayings, though only preserve "the first half" of what Origen gives us. There are a small number of sayings like this present in early Christian writings. Whether or not Jesus really said them is beyond our power to decide.

only made clear what could be asked for in good conscience would be both spiritually impoverished and distressingly one-dimensional. Origen's original audience, the elderly Christian couple Ambrose and Tatiana, could hardly be satisfied with such an un-edifying treatment of the central strand in the human attempt to reach out to God in reverence and praise. If Origen is to provide them with a reasonable portrait of prayer, he will need to treat the breadth of characters and contents it can exhibit as it tries to nourish Christian living. This is, in fact, the next topic he addresses.

Origen speaks of there being four types of prayer for which he has four different terms:[19] requests, prayers, intercessions and thanksgivings. These reflect the varied aspects of the Christian life. Origen imagines prayer affecting, and being connected to, all the elements in our lives. Our religious duties, and so our religious life, are present in all parts of our existence, if we live our religion fully, so all our moods and moments must be able to be connected to prayer. Here is what he says of the petition in the Lord's Prayer about the forgiveness of our "debts".[20]

Therefore, we are indebted, since we have certain responsibilities not only in giving but also in gentle speech and in certain kinds of deeds. Moreover, we are "indebted" to have a certain kind of disposition toward others. Since we are indebted in these ways, either we pay what is ordered by the divine Law by discharging it in full or, if we do not pay them

---

[19] These he lists on 109.
[20] sec. XXVIII.1, 147-8

because we despise the wholesome Word, we
remain in debt....there is not a single hour of
night or day in life when we are not in debt.

Origen's idea derives its logic from the conviction that
our lives are worked out in a dance of cooperation between
our own powers and inclinations and God's ruling grace.[21]

I think that God orders every rational soul
with a view to its eternal life. And the soul always
preserves free choice; and on its own responsibility it either comes to be in nobler things, ad-
vancing step by step to the summit of goods, or
descends from failing to pay attention in diverse
motions to one flood or another of evil.

This is an expression of Origen's understanding of the
'big picture' of the spiritual life. This is what he thinks is
"really going on" behind and inside the various struggles
we are aware of. This is how he understands the difficulties against which we try to fight. He is convinced that,
if we order our own actions and thoughts as we should,
to the extent we can, God will take care of the rest. His
confidence in grace is so strong that he can pause to say,
early in his treatment of the Lord's Prayer:[22]

---

[21] sec. XXIX.13, 157. As far as we can tell, this has always been
the understanding of the Greek-speaking Church and of our
brothers and sisters farther to the East. The long history of western
agonizing over the relation between divine Grace and human free
will that has bedeviled so many in the Latin tradition in the wake
of Augustine of Hippo is not an inescapable part of the Christian
landscape. A full agreement with Origen's teaching on this point
or with his manner of expressing that teaching is not required
for us to be able to benefit from his comments on this area of the
Christian struggle toward true discipleship.
[22] sec. XXII.5, 125

Therefore, let us not suppose that the Scriptures teach us to say "Our Father" at any appointed time of prayer. Rather, if we understand the earlier discussion of praying "constantly" (1 Thess. 5:17), let our whole life be a constant prayer in which we say "Our Father in heaven", and let us keep our commonwealth (Phil. 3:20) not in any way on earth, but in every way in heaven, the throne of God, because the kingdom of God is established in all those who bear the image of the Man from heaven (1 Cor. 15:49) and have thus become heavenly.

The goal of prayer, in Origen's mind, is not really to make our **prayer** better and more carefully directed. The point of prayer is that it can be a part of the remaking of our **lives**. It can be a motivating force in the raising of our lives to a higher plane, in closer communion with God, while we still live in this world. Origen wants the reader to realize how he can integrate prayer into the totality of his existence and then to start doing it. Origen is a practical author, in this work, and his goal is real, practical reformation for the Christian believer.

Chapter 4

ATHANASIUS, THE LETTER TO MARCELLINUS

It makes sense to turn from a consideration of an early Christian work on prayer to one on how to make use of the Psalter for devotion, since prayer and Scripture have always been pillars in the building of the Christian experience. *The Letter to Marcellinus* of St. Athanasius of Alexandria (ca. 295-373)[23] is the oldest surviving short treatment of how to use the Psalms as an aid to Christian devotion, and it remains one of the best. It makes sense for us to combine it with Origen's *On Prayer*, one addressing the heart of Christian Devotion and the other discussing the use of Scripture in Christian life, to get a sense of how early Christians viewed their own attempts to advance on the Christian Way. Athanasius writes a handbook on the Psalms in an attempt to help the reader understand the contents and potential usefulness of the bewilderingly various *Book of Psalms*. He wants to demonstrate that this collection has a rightful place in the Bible and that all of it can be a source of great spiritual nourishment for the Christian reader who understands its character.

This question of the place of the Psalter in the Canon of Scripture is not an idle concern on his part. Christians who sing and pray the full Psalter, rather than just a selection of greatest hits or the carefully chosen, com-

---

[23] We will use the English translation found in Gregg, Athanasius.

forting psalms that are the only ones known to so many Christians in our age, are confronted with a wide variety of moods and messages, not all of which are easy to understand. Since my own tradition takes me through the whole Psalter every month in Morning and Evening Prayer, in addition to those I meet as hymns in our hymnal or in Scripture reading and Bible Study, I am very much aware of the reality of the dismay that Athanasius is trying to allay and am glad to have his work to ponder.[24]

---

[24] It is not surprising that the well known modern work on the Psalter by C. S. Lewis, *Reflections on the Psalms*, contains three early chapters in which Lewis tries to face these challenges squarely. The modern Northern Irish Anglican and the ancient Egyptian archbishop, both intelligent and sensitive readers with a good sense of the minds and hearts of their fellows, are united in their realization that serious engagement with the Psalms must be honest, first of all.
Let me also suggest as useful reading Longman, *How to Read the Psalms* and Sarna, *On the Book of Psalms,* the first by a Christian evangelical and the second by a Jew, both religiously active academics. (see Bibliography) No treatment of Scripture can "solve" these problems (and I do not think that any treatment should "solve" them) but we all can benefit from guidance and companionship as we try to live with uncertainty and 'hard sayings' in the Bible. I am convinced that all believers are called to conform themselves to Scripture and to live their lives in the presence of God, steeping themselves in Scripture like tea bags in hot water. The water may often seem too hot for the bags to feel comfortable, but steeping in it is the only way the good that is in them can come out (and it is, after all, what tea bags are for). Athanasius' book is a treasure because he was a great theologian and a holy man and because he was fully aware of the worries that assail the devout person who approaches the Psalter with eyes and heart open. He is a good fellow Christian with whom to spend time.

Athanasius begins his discussion of the Psalter by emphasizing the unity of Scripture as coming from its connection to the one Holy Spirit.[25]

> In each book of Scripture the same things are specially declared. This report exists in all of them, and the same agreement of the Holy Spirit...in each book one is able to find prophecies and legislations and narratives. For the same Spirit is over all, and in each case in accordance with the distinction that belongs to it, each serves and fulfills the grace given to it, whether it is prophecy, or legislation, or the record of history, or the grace of the psalms.

The surface variety of the Scripture should not rob us of our sense of the underlying unity that comes from the presence and will of its divine author. This point, which is standard fare among all religious readers of Scripture, whether Jewish or Christian (though, of course, only the Christian reader would include the New Testament in his mind as he said this) is based on a religious conviction about the place of Scripture in the work of God in the world and of what God's intention in working in the world is. Without the religious belief a reader could be led to dismiss parts of the scriptural collection *in toto*. This decision, which is not uncommon in the modern West, is better understood as the expression of a religious judgment on God's action in the world than on the Bible, *per se*. My confidence in the whole Bible springs

---

[25] sec. 9, 106-107

from my experience of reading it and hearing it read and preached in worship. It is its place in my religious life that calms me when I am stumped by a 'hard saying' and I am convinced it was so for Athanasius. Only a faithful religious soul could have honestly made the declaration I have quoted for you just above.

The Psalms have an extra dimension for Athanasius beyond the general run of Scripture. They not only find their unity in their connection to the Holy Spirit and their furtherance of Its work, but they also offer believers religious assistance of a kind that the rest of Scripture cannot match, in Athanasius' opinion.[26]

> ...the Book of Psalms thus has a certain grace of its own, and a distinctive exactitude of expression....namely, that it contains even the emotions of each soul, and it has the changes and rectifications of these delineated and regulated in itself. Therefore anyone who wishes boundlessly to receive and understand from it, so as to mold himself, it is written there. For in other books one hears only what one must do and what one must not do. And one listens to the Prophets so as solely to have knowledge of the coming of the Savior. One turns his attention to the histories, on the basis of which he can know the deeds of the kings and saints. But in the Book of Psalms, the one who hears, in addition to learning these things, also comprehends and is taught in it the emotions of the soul, and, conse-

---

[26] sec. 10, 107-108

quently, on the basis of that which affects him and by which he is constrained, he also is enabled by this book to possess the image deriving from the words. Therefore, through hearing, it teaches not only to disregard passion, but also how one must heal passion through speaking and acting.

There follows on from that passage at least ten other things that Athanasius says the Psalms tell the reader how to do. This is a remarkable catalogue that shows how flexible and ever-applicable Athanasius thought the Psalter is for religious life. The connection of the Psalter with the soul makes it more readily useful for the formation of the Christian soul (and character) than the "thou shalt nots" of the other books. It does not only tell us what to do and not to do, it tells us *how* to do these things because it gives us the words with which to do them.

Athanasius does not want to say that the things that Christians had been accustomed to do with the Bible and to turn to the Bible to find could not be found in the Psalter; he specifically denies that. Athanasius does not want to seal the Psalms away from the rest of Scripture. However, he does want to say that the Psalter has dimensions of depth and usefulness that other parts of the Bible cannot match. Living at a time of Christological uproar and argument, as he did, Athanasius wants to be certain to claim the Psalter's support for the Nicene Creed. But he thinks the Psalms strike more deeply into our hearts and religious lives than just the level of the articulation of Christian teaching.[27]

---

[27] sec. 11, 109

There is also this astonishing thing in the Psalms. In the other books, those who read what the holy ones say, and what they might say concerning certain people, are relating the things that were written about those earlier people. And likewise, those who listen consider themselves to be other than those about whom the passage speaks, so that they only come to the imitation of the deeds that are told to the extent that they marvel at them and desire to emulate them. By contrast, however, he who takes up this book—the Psalter—goes through the prophecies about the Savior, as is customary in the other Scriptures, with admiration and adoration, but the other psalms he recognizes as being his own words. And the one who hears is deeply moved, as though he himself were speaking, and is affected by the words of the songs, as if they were his own songs. And for the sake of clarity of expression, do not hesitate, as the blessed Apostle says, to repeat the very things they say.

In other words, the rest of the Bible is about other people, but the Psalms are about all of us. Every believer can read them as being about him.

This way of using the Psalms as a source of our own speech in our own lives rather than as a record of the words and lives of others leads to more than just our mining the Psalter for good things to say. If we enter into the Psalms, not just in our imagination, but in our real lives, by taking the psalms out of the Bible and speaking them as our own, we are no longer just hearing the Word of God, we are also speaking It. We are turning the Word of God, expressed by the Holy Spirit, around and addressing It to God the Father as prayer. This means that we are entering into the divine life of the Trinity in a very real way.[28]

> ...after the prophecies about the Savior and the nations, he who recites the Psalms is uttering the rest as his own words, and each sings them as if they were written concerning him, and he accepts them and recites them not as if another were speaking, nor as if speaking about someone else. But he handles them as if he is speaking about himself. And the things spoken are such that he lifts them up to God as himself acting and speaking them from himself.

This opportunity to relate to the Word of God (and the words of God) from the inside rather than from the outside is not only a comfort, in Athanasius' opinion, it is also a searing challenge to the one who dares to do it.[29]

> And it seems to me that these words become like a mirror to the person singing them, so that he might perceive himself and the emotions of his soul, and thus affected, he might recite them. For in fact he who hears the one reading receives the song that is re-

[28] sec. 11, 110
[29] sec. 12, 111

45

cited as being about him, and either, when he is convicted by his conscience, being pierced, he will repent, or hearing of the hope that resides in God, and of the succor available to believers—how this kind of grace exists for him—he exults and begins to give thanks to God....And so, on the whole, each psalm is both spoken and composed by the Spirit so that in these same words, as was said earlier, the stirrings of our souls might be grasped, and all of them be said as concerning us, and the same issue from us as our own words, for a remembrance of the emotions in us, and a chastening of our life.

Not only, then, are we given in the Psalter words to say to God that are fitting and holy, but these words themselves, because they are divine, pierce us to the heart and show us our true worth. Not only are we given words to use to call out to God in our time of trouble, but the depth and seriousness of our predicament is made known to us by these same words.[30] As is always true in the religious life, the clearer our knowledge of ourselves and of God becomes, the greater is our sense of the gulf between us and Him and of our unworthiness of Him. The challenge we discover as we come to see these things more clearly in the Psalms also brings its own answer by giving us a way to address God in our audacity. If it is true to say, as Athanasius does,[31]

---

[30] Psalm 69 is a good example of this.
[31] sec. 30, 126

> For I believe that the whole of human ex-
> istence, both the dispositions of the soul and
> the movements of the thoughts, have been
> measured out and encompassed in those very
> words of the Psalter.

then speaking these words in our life is putting that life in its proper place. That means that the proper place for our life is in the midst of God's relation to the world, of which the Bible is an instance and a record, and in the midst of the human approach to God and attempt to understand and serve Him that the Bible exists to support. It means that putting our lives in their proper place is putting our life into a divine context. What could be more sanctifying than to put our lives, consciously, in the presence of God?

Athanasius' conviction that this understanding of the Psalter and how to use it is correct is shown in his idea of the benefit of using these words as prayer. He is not appealing to this idea as an interesting thought or as one that is a stepping-off place for a Christian's imagination, he puts it forward as being a true description of the nature of the Psalter and of the way in which God intends us to use His gift. The following passage makes clear that the use of the scriptural words by a believer carries with it a responsibility as well as an opportunity, which is always the case when great and expansive openings are presented to us. The opportunity provides wide-reaching possibilities if the responsibility is met with care.[32]

---

[32] sec. 31, 127

Do not let anyone amplify these words of the Psalter with the persuasive phrases of the profane, and do not let him attempt to recast or completely change the words. Rather let him recite and chant, without artifice, the things written just as they were spoken, in order for the holy men who supplied these, recognizing that which is their own, to join you in your prayer, or, rather, so that even the Spirit who speaks in the saints, seeing words inspired by him in them, might render assistance to us.

So, in Athanasius' picture, the Psalter shows us what to do, helps us do it, takes us into the life of God and places our prayers together with those of the saints gone before us and those of the Holy Ghost. We can pray together with the Paraclete and take comfort in the presence of the Comforter when we pray the Psalms, because they are His words as well as ours. We are praying with the Spirit as much as the Spirit is praying with us when we are praying the Psalter.

In both of these pictures of religious life that come down to us from the early centuries of Christian living, the pursuit of the Christian life is seen as something that hallows human life and brings it close to (and into) God the Father. Religious life is all-encompassing in Origen's view because it needs to take all of our lives in it for it to reach its full potential. Religious life in Athanasius' picture is all-encompassing on even a higher level because it takes us up into the divine life and so, automatically, connects us to all of Creation through connecting us to the Creator of all. Whether viewed from the point of view of an examination of our life and daily concerns, as Origen does, or from the point of view of pointing out the connection between our religious activities and the life of God, as Athanasius does, both these ancient Christians present pictures of religious life that imagine no part of our existence that should (or could) be left out of it. The understanding of what serious Christian devotion entails is a demanding one, in both Origen's and Athanasius' pictures, but the possible rewards for persevering in it are even more extravagant than the demands. Neither of these teachers is promising what is sometimes called "cheap grace" but both are promising untold richness of blessings for the believer who clings to God. Their very different points of focus have resulted in pictures that fit together very completely.

Chapter 5

APHRAHAT AND THE COVENANTERS

Now let us turn to consider the "Sons and Daughters of the Covenant" in the Middle Eastern realm of the early Church. Although the Church outside the Roman Empire is almost completely absent from the imaginations of western Christians it was a large and vibrant body for much of Christian history and it endures to the present day. This branch of our Christian family has much to teach us all if we will only take the time to sit and listen.[33] Sometimes looking at Christians whose practical situations were very different from our own can help us not only to learn about their understanding of the Faith but also about our own. When we see our own most deeply held convictions expressed (and lived) by people so far from us we can gain a truer understanding of the character and meaning of these beliefs and so can hope to be better able to live them out in our own lives.

We should note, as we begin, that when we hear of these intensely dedicated Christians, they are already an existing group in the Church. They enter into the historical record full formed, as it were, and we do not know

---

[33] Paul S. Russell, "Syriac Christianity" and Moffett, *Christianity in Asia* are two places to start. Gilman and Klimkeit offer a treatment that is more theological as well as historical. Much more is easily available in English on this subject than was the case even ten years ago. I encourage anyone who is interested to begin looking into this area of Christian history. A wealth of delights and spiritual sustenance awaits you!

their time of origin. The "Sons and Daughters of the Covenant" seem to be a native sprig of the Syrian Church that predated the rise of the much more famous Egyptian monasticism.

Syrian Christians have been well known from the early days of the Church for their tendency to pursue ascetical live. At present, many scholars think it likely that the peculiar cultural background of the Syrian Church played a large role in nurturing this style of life. The following passage can serve as a representative of that view:[34]

> Doubtless enough has already been said to alert the reader to the peculiarly ascetical tone of Christianity in Syria and Palestine. As one author summed up the situation:
>> 'Early Syriac Christianity is permeated with asceticism.'
>
> It would seem probable that much of this had its roots in various Jewish groups like the Essenes, but there does seem to have been something of a propensity for mortification and fasting within the Syrian spirit long before the appearance of Christianity
>
>> 'The same psyche which was formerly devoted to pre-Christian deities, was now placed at the disposal of the aims of Christian asceticism.'

So the soil itself, within the Syrian countryside, was receptive to such seed.

---

[34] Gillman and Klimkeit, *Christians in Asia,* 52

We should realize that this ascetic urge was not just a product of the imaginations of Christians in the Syriac-speaking world, rather, it was a response to how this wing of the Church read the Bible and heard it challenge them to live. This call to asceticism that they heard in Scripture played directly into how some of them viewed marriage's place in the Christian life. Their understanding of marriage is one of the most famous facts about the early Syrian Christians, so we ought to consider it as a part of our examination of the Sons and Daughter of the Covenant.[35]

> The other subject on which the Gospels gave no explicit teaching was that of marriage. I say 'explicit' advisedly, for the early Syriac-speaking church thought otherwise. One passage in particular evidently caught their attention, and once again it is interesting to see the ascetic slant that Luke, alone of the Synoptics, provides. The passage in question is Luke xx 35-6, with parallels in Matthew xx 30 and Mark xii 25. Jesus is answering the Saduccees' query about resurrection, and in the course of Jesus' reply in Matthew and Mark we find the words: "At the resurrection men and women do not marry; they are like angels in heaven". In Luke, on the other hand, there is a significant difference: "Those who have been judged worthy of a place in the other world, and of the resurrection from the dead, do not marry, for they are not sub-

[35] Brock, "Early Syrian Asceticism", 5-6

ject to death any longer. They are like angels; they are sons of God, because they share in the resurrection". In other words, the worthy *already* anticipate the marriageless life of angels *in this world*. The implications are even clearer in the Old Syriac translation of the passage: "Those who have become worthy to receive that world (i.e. the kingdom) and that resurrection from the dead, do not marry, nor can they die, for they have been made equal with the angels, (and being) the sons of the resurrection (they are) like the sons of God".

The effect this stern picture of the ideal life had on the Christians in the Syriac-speaking world was profound. Many of them could not leave this challenge unmet and still be confident that they were dedicating themselves to the life of the Gospel. So, at some time before our records begin, there arose within the Church a group that exhibited a special dedication to the Faith, including an ascetical response to the matter of how to fit marriage into the Christian life. The Syrian Church was convinced that their special dedication to virtue showed that these people were worthy of the charitable support and spiritual respect of the larger Christian community. This idea of a special sub-group within the Body of Christ was one

---

[36] These two brief quotations are drawn from Griffith, 'Singles', 146-147 and Griffith, "Asceticism", 222, respectively. The connection of their lives with Scripture was an important point for these Christians and is an important point for us to keep in mind as we look back at them.

that had, of course, been present in the Church from the time of the New Testament.[36]

> ...*Ihidaye* occupied a position comparable to that assigned to widows and virgins already in the New Testament and in early ecclesiastical books of canons.

> ...crucial texts by Aphrahat, "the Persian Sage" (died c. 345 CE) and Ephraem the Syrian allow one a glimpse of the lifestyle within the church of Syria of communities of "singles" in God's service, whose way of life is parallel to that of the biblical widows and virgins and with whom the men and women "singles" will be bracketed in later canonical legislation.

More than just an order that, in some way, hearkened back to the pure days of the first Christians, the "Covenanters"[37] were also, in a manner in tune with the most enthusiastic Christian strains of thought, looking forward to the Second Coming of the Messiah as well.[38]

> In fourth-century Syriac writers we find the idea that the baptismal life of all Christians should ideally anticipate the resurrection life, which will represent the marriageless life of angels.

---

[37] Nedungatt aptly calls them this in his article. I will use his term, generally, as a matter of convenience.
[38] Brock, *Spirituality,* 56-57 and 54

It is very likely that both Aphrahat and
Ephrem were ihidaye/bnay qyama,[1] and many
of their works were addressed specifically to fellow ihidaye. As a result they speak very highly
of the ideal of virginity and qaddishutha.[2] This
has led some modern scholars to suppose that
they held a very low view of marriage, and that
this was partly a result of a dualistic view of the
world which regarded sexuality as something
essentially evil. This interpretation is extremely misguided, and finds no support in what
Aphrahat and Ephrem actually say; indeed,
when Aphrahat gives examples of 'virginity'
and 'qaddishutha' from the Old Testament,
these are often cases where these states are seen
as a period of preparation. The same idea of
qaddishutha as a period of preparation can
be seen in Ephrem's Commentary on Genesis
chapter 8:

> And God said to Noah, 'Go out, you and
> your wife, your sons and your sons' wives'
> (Gen. 8:16). Those whom God had caused to
> come in singly, to preserve qaddishutha in the
> Ark, He caused to leave in couples, in order to
> multiply and be fruitful in creation. He also
> said concerning the animals which had pre-
> served qaddishutha in the ark, 'Take out with
> you every animal that was with you...and let

---

[1] The first word is what Griffith translates as 'singles' and the
second phrase means 'sons of the Covenant'. (author's note)
[2] This Syriac word mean "holiness". (author's note)

them give birth on the earth and be fruitful and multiply on it' (Gen, 8:17-18) (Comm. On Genesis VI.12)

This idea of virginity and qaddishutha as preparation provides a pointer to one of the main motivating forces which led people to undertake these ascetic vows at baptism, namely the concept of Christ as the heavenly Bridegroom…

This urge to shape their lives apart from marriage in anticipation of the arrival of the fullness of God's Kingdom was also supported by a strong desire to imitate Jesus' life in their own, which can fairly be called the most traditional and scriptural of Christian ideas.[41] The importance of this attachment of the Christian understanding of religious life to the person and example of Jesus cannot be over-estimated. Christians have always felt that the more closely they could model their lives on Jesus the truer and better Christians (and human beings) they would be. Griffith discusses this aspect of the self-understanding of the Covenanters at some length. Much of this connection stems from the fact that the term *Ihidaya* (single, only, alone), which the Covenanters used to refer to themselves, was a scriptural title and description of Jesus in the Syriac Bible.[42]

---

[41] It is present, very clearly, in *Philippians* 2 in St. Paul's use of the hymn he quotes there.

[42] Griffith, 'Singles', 148, 149, 153, 155-156. I have tried to put enough short citations together for you so that you can see Griffith's point clearly.

For in Syriac religious texts the term is
not simply a designation for a Christian ascetic of some sort, it is first of all a title of
Christ with Biblical authority, and this is its
primary point of reference for many Syriac
writers.

...in Syriac ascetical texts the denotation
of the term *Ihidaya* is not limited to the no-
tion of the 'singleness' that bespeaks first of
all, celibacy or religious bachelorhood. Rather, it includes the element of singleness of
purpose (monotropos), along with the clear
claim that a person called 'single' for ascetical
reasons is thereby also said to be in a special
relationship with Jesus the Christ, the "Single
One', the single son of God the Father (John
1:14, 18, 3:16, 18). And this latter sense of
the term may have been the primary one for
the Syrians.

...the very synonymy of the titles in
Ephraem's ecclesial community bespeaks a
special relationship between Christ and the
celibate ascetic that is instinct in the very
term that designates them both.

...the Syriac term *Ihidaya*, unlike the
Greek term *monachos* which shares part of its
range of meaning, is a scriptural term that in
Christian usage applies first of all to Christ
himself, with the full set of connotations that

only the several Greek words used to interpret it will allow the non-Syriac speaker to discern. Secondly, in Syriac, this term was also used by writers such as Aphrahat and Ephraem to designate the so-called 'ascetics' in the community, precisely because the intention of these ascetic celibates was publicly to 'put on' the *persona* of the *Ihidaya* from the bosom of the Father. Their purpose was to imitate Christ.

The goal of the life the Covenanters were attempting to lead seems clear now: they were trying to imitate Jesus, but the question that ought to interest us the most still remains: "How did these urges express themselves on the practical level? What did the Covenanters actually do?"

We have one early Christian work addressed to those who practiced this form of life, written by Aphrahat (actively writing from before 337 to 345), a Christian living beyond the bounds of the Roman world in Persia to the East.[43] The contents of this work are not entirely intelligible to us, so little do we know about its time and place of origin, nor is it the kind of systematic piece a modern writer would be trained to produce. Still, we can get an

---

[43] This work, called his "Sixth Demonstration", is available in English in more than one place. The easiest one for most readers to find will be the one listed in the Bibliography as Aphrahat, Selections. A more recent translation that is easier on the eye is Aphrahat, Demonstrations I. This second translation does not yet contain all of Aphrahat's work, but a second volume is reported to be on its way.

outline of the lives of the Covenanters from it, clearly enough.

Nedungatt describes them as follows, in a section of his article that he calls "Aphrahat's Rule".[44]

†

> Before all things, it beseems the man on whom the yoke is laid, that his faith should be firm...that he should be zealous in fasting and prayer; that he should be fervent in the love of Christ; and should be humble and mild and wise.

†

> And let his speech be peaceful and pleasant and his thought be sincere with all. Let him speak his words duly weighing them, and set a barrier to his mouth from harmful words, and let him put far from him hasty laughter.

---

[44] Nedungatt, 425-428. This kind of systematization of Aphrahat is sometimes criticized by scholars who say that turning Aphrahat's very unsystematic disquisition into something palatable to a modern western mind is a way of deforming it. While I am also conscious of a concern that we should not domesticate Aphrahat into a neat example of something that comforts us, I do think that organizing his presentation in order to see it more clearly is a legitimate technique to aid our understanding. Aphrahat's writing is shapeless, to our modern western eyes, and we will save much time and effort by letting Nedungatt simplify our task. My citations will pick out the details that Nedungatt puts forward as worthy of note. The words cited are the words of Aphrahat as Nedungattt gives them, but I have omitted some of these on account of space constraints and from a desire to simplify things. The crosses mark divisions between separate citations from Nedungatt.

†

Let him not love the adornment of garments nor again does it become him to let his hair grow long and adorn it, or to anoint it with sweet-scented unguents.

†

Let him not recline at feastings nor does it become him to wear gorgeous apparel; let him not dare to exceed at wine. Let him put far from him proud thoughts; it does not become him to eye [lit. "to look upon" Gwynn] the gorgeous apparel, or to wear fine raiment.

†

Let him put away from him a crafty tongue; let him drive from him envy and wrath and cast away from him crafty lips. The words that are spoken about a man, when he about whom they are spoken is not near, let him not hear nor receive, that he sin not, until he search them out. Mockery is a hateful fault, and to bring it up upon the heart is not right.

†

Let him not lend and take interest, and let him not love avarice; let him [rather] suffer wrong and not do wrong.

†

Furthermore, let him put away from him turmoil, and words of jesting let him not utter. Let him not scorn any man who is repenting of his sins. And let him not mock his brother who is fasting, and him that cannot fast let him not put to shame.

†

Let him not speak with complaisance with a wicked man, nor with his enemy. And so let him contend as to have no enemy at all. When men envy him in that which is good, let him add to his goodness and let him not be harmed because of envy.

†

When he has and gives to the poor let him rejoice; when he has not, let it not grieve him.

†

With a wicked man let him have no converse and with a contemptuous man let him not speak, lest he give himself to contempt. With a blasphemer let him not dispute, lest his Lord be blasphemed on his account. Let him depart from a slanderer, and let no man please another man with speciousness of words.

†

These things beseem solitaries who take up the heavenly yoke, and become disciples of Christ. For thus it befits the disciples of Christ to be like unto Christ their Master.

The closing statement shows clearly that Aphrahat understands this whole set of guidelines as aids in imitating Christ. Aphrahat's intention is to help his fellows see clearly how that imitation of Christ can best be done.

The first thing that comes to my mind on reading these directives is that this is not a pattern of life that seems far-fetched or impossible to us. Celibacy, we have already seen, was understood as an anticipation of angelic life and we might respect that intention without wishing to engage in it ourselves, but the rest of these rules for living seem firmly and sanely anchored in the pursuit of finding a Christian pattern of life on the earth that will help along the coming of the Kingdom. This fact should make us think again about how we view early Christian practice, and so should the particular directives that Athanasius feels necessary to set down.

Modern western Christians are so far from the trials and uncertainties of our ancestors in the Faith that we often view them as being completely different creatures than we are. We credit them with super-human devotion, with super-human sanctity and with less than the usual human tendency to settle for worldly living with a Christian face. This group of the Sons and Daughters of the Covenant should disabuse us of our false ideas.

These rules would only have been necessary for people who were not successfully acting this way already. People who are already dressing in a restrained manner are not exhorted to have a modest appearance. Those who never over-indulge are not instructed to be moderate in eating and drinking. Those who are tractable and eager to help their fellows are not told to be ready to give and receive religious instruction. These rules show that the Covenanters were Christians who had decided to set themselves the task of living more completely Christian lives, but it does not show that they were people who succeeded at that task. When we remember that the Covenanters were those in the Syrian Church who had set themselves with particular fervor to pursuing the Christian ideal, we will be more convinced that all Christians, in all ages, face the same trials and temptations. Their fervor did not make them immune to the failings that we know in ourselves. Their willingness to take on a serious attempt to live good Christian lives is what separates these earlier Christians from us. We have no reason to think of them as great spiritual successes (Aphrahat certainly did not or he would not have produced these instructions for them) and we do them, and ourselves, a disservice if we do. The Covenanters longed to be good and were making an effort to advance in their religious lives but they were not creatures set apart from us. Both their faults and their virtues have more akin to us in them than ought to make either of us comfortable.

Concluding Summary

So, this overview in these brief chapters has shown us that there were a variety of ways in which believers who lived earlier in the Christian stream than our central examples embarked on serious religious living. We have seen that Scripture (the Psalms) offered examples of both success and failure in this endeavor and that early Christians discussed the deepening of the believer's religious life in prayer (Origen), through the study of Scripture (Athanasius) and by living the Christian life according to a set pattern (the Covenanters). The knowledge we have acquired will allow us to engage with the Desert dwellers of Egypt and the Poor Man of Assisi with a better understanding of how they were breaking new ground and how they were following the footsteps of saints who had gone before them.

While our main subjects may seem very novel to us, it would be a misunderstanding if we thought that they were really doing something that had not been tried before. We have moved from the heart of the religious stream (Psalms 1 and 15), to those believers who were serious enough to want to enquire into the nature of Prayer and to learn how to study and use the Psalms more successfully, and now we are leaving the ordinary believer behind to look at the examples set us by some of the most extraordinary Christians who have yet lived. We should let the fervent, but flawed, Covenanters serve as a bridge between the teaching of Origen and Athanasius and the lives of the Desert Monks.

We now move several hundred miles to the south-west, from western Persia to Egypt, from the larger world to the Roman Empire, and begin our visit to the Desert ascetics of Egypt. They will make the Syrian Covenanters seem very tame, indeed.

THE DESERT FATHERS OF EGYPT

Chapter 6

INTRODUCTION[45]

There came to the abbot Joseph the abbot Lot, and said to him, "Father, according to my strength I keep a modest rule of prayer and fasting and meditation and quiet, and according to my strength I purge my imagination: what more must I do?" The old man, rising, held up his hands against the sky, and his fingers became like ten torches of fire, and he said, "If thou wilt, thou shalt be made wholly a flame."[46]

Let me try to give you a brief background sketch of the Desert tradition from Egypt so you will not be distracted from the content of these stories by the exotic locale in which they take place and their distance from us in time. Keep your eyes on the spiritual strivings of the figures in the stories and the principles they teach.

---

[45] I have tried to use the word "Desert" capitalized, to refer to the Desert movement or the particular areas in which the early monks lived, as opposed to the "desert", which would be the harsh environment in which they lived. This is not neat, but it does reflect the way in which people have customarily discussed this topic. Thus, according to this way of speaking, the Desert Fathers moved out into the desert surrounding Egypt in order to have the space and freedom to pursue the life they thought was their calling.

[46] viii/117 in Waddell. All passages of Desert literature are drawn from Waddell unless otherwise noted.

At their heart, these stories come out of the same urge to live their lives as followers of Jesus that we have already seen evidence of in the believers of the earliest Christian centuries and that Christians still feel today.

Early in the fourth century A.D., that is, early in the 300s, as we count years these days, there arose among Christians a movement of great force that spread from Egypt, primarily, and from the Middle East, secondarily, throughout the Christian world. People began leaving their homes and families in growing numbers and setting out into the world to live lives separated from family and normal society in an attempt to draw closer to God. The Covenanters are evidence that a desire among Christians to lead what we now call "religious" lives, that is, lives governed by formal rules, existed earlier than this, but this explosion of membership and influence was unprecedented and quite surprising. The first hundred years or so of this movement have not only set the tone for the many different sorts of Christian communities that would come after them in the history of the Church down to the present day, but also have served as inspiration and instruction for Christians of all kinds who have sought to live intelligent, dedicated Christian lives. (I am not a monk, and I have never been a monk, and, since I am married with three children, it looks as though I never will be a monk, but I think that the Desert Fathers have something to say to me, nonetheless, and I would like to try to show you some of what the Desert dwellers thought and why I think they are worth our consideration.)

There is an ocean of material on the first hundred years of the desert monks. (Monk, it is worth saying again, is a word that applies to both men and women.

It means someone living alone, outside a family group. From the very beginning of this movement there have been women involved in it, which is something that the movement's literature has described in detail. This is not a new discovery or something that Christians have sought to down-play, though modern book publishers, in their desire to sell their wares, often advertise books about female ascetics as unexpected discoveries.) Scholars argue over many things about the Desert Fathers.

The study of the Desert Fathers is a special area requiring special work and special preparation and it is not my own field. (We are all amateurs here, in this project. We are studying these things for the love of them rather than as our work.) Still, reading the works about the Desert Fathers and by the Desert Fathers has been a standard part of a literate Christian life for 17 centuries, so what we are doing is not unusual but, in fact, very traditional.

The Desert Literature was written with us in mind: it was written by the monks for those who couldn't visit the Desert and ask the great teachers for advice, but who still wanted to learn from their teaching. What we will do in these chapters is not only a traditional thing to do, it is what the Desert Fathers themselves hoped we would do with their writings. We are reading the stories of the teachers of the Desert in hopes that they will help us improve our religious lives. This is the most common way of approaching this material ever since it was produced.

Every ancient Christian language contains large amounts of material springing from the Desert movement. Scholars have spent lifetimes trying to figure out how these different traditions and different documents are connected. I can save you 20 years of work by telling you that, at present, we cannot know how all these writings fit together and we probably never will. There is so much of this material that a great deal of it has never been read by modern people and remains only in manuscripts in libraries in the Middle East and elsewhere. However, this is good news for us because it means that, like our brothers and sisters gone before, when we take up books about the Desert Fathers and read, we are connecting ourselves to a living, multi-form tradition that was created with us in mind and exists to help us do what we are trying to do: that is, to live better Christian lives.

Since no one knows where to begin in reading the Desert Fathers, we are going to do what everyone must do: just jump in the ocean and splash around. The best, and most enjoyable, approach is to read many pages of sayings, some organized by topic and some not, and just let them wash over you as you live with them for a while. The goal is to spend as much time with the tales of the Desert as we can: reading them, thinking about them and talking about them. Of the particular stories that I have chosen to use as illustrations, some will make sense to you right away, some will take some time to come into focus and will become clear as we progress and some may never be clear to us. That is all right. You will see that many of the monks, themselves, were often at a loss in the stories we will read. I hope that what you read as you move through these chapters will spur you to take a look at one or more of the other books on the list of books about the Desert ascetics contained in the Bibliography. I have put some brief comments of my own on the list to help you choose books that will pique your interest and answer your questions. I have tried to include collections of material translated into English, as well as modern studies of the Desert Fathers, so that you

could balance a direct connection with them with some
secondary explanations of what they said and what they
did. Some of the collections that survive are just random
collections of sayings. Some of the collections that survive are organized, with the sayings grouped together under the name of the person thought to have pronounced
them and then with these groups gathered together, usually in alphabetical order.[47] So, when one is approaching
the Desert Fathers, reading from collections of sayings, as
we will do, is not a disorganized approach. It is the most
usual one for people of all periods.

One of the things to keep in mind as you read is
that we are never certain how the sayings we read relate
to what the people involved actually said and did. This
problem cannot be solved because of the limits of what
we now know. Do not ask if any particular story is true or
if any saying was really spoken by the person it is credited
to; we do not, and cannot, know. Besides, the Desert Tradition repeats stories because of their value for teaching,
not as an historical record of the movement. What we can
know about the monks of the desert is what they believed

---

[47] This, in itself, is a hint that the material's organization is not
original, because organizing things alphabetically is a Western
idea. You may have noticed that, in the Bible, writings grouped
together are commonly grouped with the longest writing first.
The prophets in the Old Testament work this way as do the letters
of St. Paul in the New Testament. This is the traditional way of
organizing written material in the Middle East. It is the way the
Koran is organized, which is one of the reasons why the Koran is
so difficult for non-Muslims to use. (There were western people
interested in this material from the very beginning and Latin
language collections of Desert sayings can be very ancient, but
the process of setting them down is, already, to a certain extent,
taking them out of their natural habitat.)

and what they taught. We cannot know what they did, as a matter of history, because they were not interested in themselves and they did not record their own history, as we think of history today. There are, also, not the sort of un-biased, outside accounts of them that modern western historians love. Since they lived away from the usual areas of human habitation in Egypt, the monks usually came into contact only with those who sought them out. These were people looking for the monks so they could profit from their wisdom and be close to their sanctity. The writings that these people produced have become much of the Desert literature we have to read, but they do not serve as an external source for scholars to use to evaluate other parts of the ascetical writings of the Desert. The only dependable use that we can make of their writings is the one for which they were created: to come to grips with the challenge of the life they taught themselves and each other to lead.

The saying with which I began this chapter is a prime example of this and one of my favorite sayings of the Desert Fathers. It is unclear to me whether the person who reported that saying was trying to tell us that the hands of Abba[48] Joseph really became flames, physically,

---

[48] Traditionally, Desert monks were called "Abba" ("father") and "Amma" ("mother") as a sign of respect for their superior knowledge and sanctity. This was not because they were ordained ministers in the Church. Almost all of the monks were lay people and wished to remain so. (Members of religious orders are still lay people today, though it is much more common for them also to be ordained.)
When a character in a story is called "Abba" or "old man", we are meant to understand that that person is being credited with spiritual wisdom and is thought of as a good source of spiritual advice.

or not. Many of the sayings of the Desert Fathers and stories about them contain miracles. Sometimes, it seems clear to me that we are being given what claim to be historical records of miraculous happenings, but, sometimes, I am not so sure. That question, though, is beside the point. The stories in the Desert literature are reported because they are thought to be helpful. They should be read with that in mind. Trying to sort out the historical record of the monastic movement is not our task. Over the next few chapters, we are going to try to get a few glimpses into the minds and hearts of the early Desert monks. We should read all these stories with a desire to discover what they teach and to discover what we think of that teaching. The question of whether these stories are all historical is not relevant to our concerns or to why the Desert literature hands them down to us.

As you read, it is important for you to keep a few things in mind:

First, you should be aware that the early Desert monks supported themselves with manual labor. We know this both from the stories told about them and from archaeological excavation. Many stories make no mention of this, but it is always assumed. The monks were not looked after by large, global institutions of the

---

Waddell translates this word as "Abbot" in her volume, which is a serious error, I believe. Abbot is, of course, closely related to "Abba", but it carries with it the picture of someone who ruled over a large and highly organized monastic establishment in the Middle Ages, which is exactly what the Egyptian monks did not want to do.

When I refer to a person in my own words I will use "Abba" but I have left Waddell's translation as it stands. Careful readers will make sure to remind themselves not to think of grand French clerics when they see "abbot" appear in these stories.

sort that western Christian religious orders have become today. They risked life and limb, as well as comfort, to undertake their religious quest. They were pioneers of the body as well as of the spirit, living on the edge of the civilized world and the edge of Christian religious experience.

Second, notice how the monks try to balance a desire for solitary contemplation with participation in group worship and the practice of Christian charity. The stories about the Desert Fathers involving the hospitality they offered to each other, and to travelers and to visitors, number in the hundreds, but, mostly by chance, we will see very few of them. We should always keep in mind that this hospitable socializing was a constant element in their lives.

Third, think of the desert dwellers as dedicated Christian seekers. If we dwell on the practical particulars of their lives, we make them seem so far away from us that they have nothing in common with us and nothing to tell us, and that is a great mistake.

That brings us to a foundational question. Why did they go out into the desert to seek God? The short answer is that they went out there because John the Baptist went out there and Jesus went out there and they felt that God was there and that, out there, they could be alone with Him. They went to the desert so they would be able to seek God without distractions or interruptions. The harsh nature of the desert setting bears witness to their seriousness of purpose. No one goes into the Egyptian desert for fun.

Many of us tell ourselves that we long to be alone with God, if only we had the time to do so. Many of us tell ourselves that we long to be alone with God, if only our lives allowed it. The question is: do we make time in our lives to allow us to seek God?

One of the things I want us to keep in mind is that the desert dwellers we will be studying never gave up their attempts to be alone with God, even as there grew to be great crowds around the oases in the desert. One of the greatest differences between the Desert monks and me is that their dedication to seeking the face of God was much greater than my own is. The differences in my daily life and theirs pale in comparison to this one great, central difference. They acted on their desire for God in a way that I, at least so far, never have. That is what we should reflect on as we move through these chapters and that is the challenge that we should take with us as we move on to the later parts of this book.

> Be present, O merciful God, and protect us through the silent hours of this night, so that we, who are fatigued by the changes and chances of this fleeting world, may repose upon thy eternal changelessness, through the everlasting Christ our Lord. Amen.[49]

---

[49] #223, 77, in Fisher

Chapter 7

PRAYER AND ATTENTION

> O Perfect Love, who art the light of the world, light thou this day for us, and unto this end create and confirm the habit of lovingkindness in our hearts, of prayer in our minds, that we may set thee as the sun in the centre of our lives, through Jesus Christ who loveth us. Amen.[50]

Religious life is life lived in an awareness of the presence of God, so prayer is a natural part of it and attention to prayer is a necessary element in religious life. Prayer is also one of the most central elements in the lives of the early Desert Fathers, so any Christian person interested in prayer and how to practice it would do well to look at them to see if they offer us a useful example to follow in our lives, today.

The common practice of the early Desert Fathers was to engage in a daily round of prayers and recitation of psalms in their individual cells, or huts. Their individual prayer was supplemented by attendance at a weekly Eucharist shared in common by all the monks living in a particular place. This balance of religious practice between individual and corporate worship is one that has never been common in the Western Church, even among monastic groups. It shows that the lives pursued by the

---

[50] #218, 73, in Fisher

Desert Fathers were an interesting mix of an hermetic approach[51] and a corporate approach. This explains some of the freedom of practice that we see reflected in the stories that we read about them.

As a general rule, each monk made an effort to live the best life he could, in his own cell. They thought of their vocation as a solitary vocation and many of the teaching stories we will look at reflect that reality. What this means, of course, is that our own Christian lives can be placed more closely in parallel with theirs since there is an irreducible individual aspect to our Christian lives, too. As individuals, looking at the individual Desert Fathers, we find ourselves watching other Christians who are grappling with the same problems that often trouble us as we think about the daily practice of our religious lives.

It is not surprising that the question of how to fit prayer into one's life was one of the central concerns of people who had set themselves to live lives of prayer. The Desert Fathers were well aware of how difficult it is to try to live a life that really is made up of unceasing prayer.

> There came to the abbot Lucius in Enna certain monks of the kind called Euchitae, that is, the Men of Prayer: and the old man asked them saying, "What kind of handiwork do ye do?" And they said, "We touch no kind of handiwork, but as the Apostle says, we pray without ceasing." The old man said to them, "So ye do not eat?" They said, "Yea, we

---

[51] That is, the approach of hermits, who live by themselves and try to spend their time alone.

eat." And the old man said, "Now while ye
are eating, who prays for you?" And again he
questioned them, saying, "Ye do not sleep?"
And they said, "We sleep." And the old man
said, "And while ye sleep, who prays for you?"
And they could find no answer.

And he said to them, "Forgive me, my
brethren, but behold ye do not do as ye have
said: but I shall show you how in working
with my hands, I pray without ceasing. For
I sit, by the help of God, steeping my few
palm-leaves and from them I weave a mat
and I say, 'Have mercy upon me, O God, according to thy loving-kindness: according to
the multitude of thy tender mercies blot out
my transgressions.'"[52] And he said to them,
"Is this a prayer or no?" And they said to him,
"Yea." And he said, "When I abide all the day
working and praying with heart and mouth, I
make sixteen denarii more or less, and out of
them I leave two at the door, and I spend the
rest on food. But whoso finds the two denarii prays for me while I eat and sleep: and so
by God's grace there is fulfilled in me as the
Scripture saith, 'Pray without ceasing.'"[53]

Here, in this lovely story, we find many of the strains
of thought that surface in the stories of the Desert Fathers
when they discuss prayer. They take to heart St. Paul's
admonition to "pray without ceasing"[54], but they realize
that, on a literal level, it is impossible. Each of them is

---

[52] *Psalm* 51:1
[53] ix, 117-118
[54] *1 Thessalonians* 5:17

striving to live a perfect Christian life, but this command of St. Paul makes them realize that it is impossible for an individual person to do this on his own. What this story shows us is the care and intelligence with which the Desert Fathers approached the task of living a Christian life. They did not allow themselves to be blinded by their original sense of vocation into settling for something that was less than satisfactory. There was in most of them a deep urge to be perfect, **as individuals**, but they realized, through trial and error, that they could not do this. So, they picked themselves up and began to try to live their solitary vocation in community. This story is one of the best known in the Desert tradition because it describes the creation of a community of prayer by one of the monks as a part of his attempt to be a perfect Christian.

It is not just the case that some kind of community is necessary for the individual to succeed in prayer, though. We must see clearly that the story teaches that prayer is made perfect by **charity**. The individual's religious life cannot be complete if it does not include care for others. Thus, we see that this story runs parallel to the parable of the Good Samaritan, in its own way.[55] Both the monks in this tale and the priest and Levite in the parable are engaged in their own religious observances. The monk succeeds as a religious person because he includes charitable acts in his life and the priest and Levite, like the Men of Prayer in the story, fail because they place their observances before practical charity.

One of the ironies of this great mass movement of people attempting to live Christianity as solitaries is that they discovered that, in order to be perfect Christians,

---

[55] *Luke* 10: 25-37

they had to be part of a community. This is a lesson that we modern Americans could well take to heart since it works against our cultural predisposition to individuality, in all ways and at all times. If even the Desert monks, who flung themselves fully into their attempt to live up to the Christian religious ideal, came, in the end, to the conclusion that they needed others to help them if they were to succeed, then we should take their conclusion seriously. We need our brothers and sisters in the Church at the same time that we need God. We cannot reach Him without each other's help.

Let us turn to another word from one of the greatest spiritual teachers of the early Desert. This also relates to prayer, but comes at the topic through discussing what can impede it.

> The abbot Macarius said, "If we dwell upon the harms that have been wrought on us by men, we amputate from our mind the power of dwelling upon God."[56]

In this saying, we see reflected one of the most common difficulties that we have with our prayers. Human beings have a tendency to dwell on their own concerns, especially on areas in which we think we have been wronged. This allows us both to feel virtuous for having been wronged and to reflect on the shortcomings of others, which we always find both amusing and encouraging. (Remember the story told by Jesus in which the Pharisee takes time out from his prayer to thank God for not having made him like the tax-collector standing next to him.[57] He is a very representative figure. Even if we can

---

[56] xxxiv, 107
[57] *Luke* 18:9-14

keep those sentiments from our lips during our prayers, keeping them out of our hearts as we move through the day is a much more difficult thing.) Instead of prayer being a conversation between us and God and a chance for us to draw ourselves closer to Him, we find that it often becomes an opportunity for us to denigrate others before Him and to entertain thoughts of our superiority to the people who have wronged us. All these are distractions and all are enemies of spiritual progress and closeness to God. The Desert Fathers knew this temptation also and worked long and hard at training themselves to focus during prayer on the purpose of the prayer and not to be distracted by other questions and side issues.

It is not only true, however, that we can get in the way of our prayers while we are performing them. It is also the case that, after our worship is completed, we can render null the benefits we might enjoy from it because of our behavior as we depart. Another story makes this point quite clearly.[58] Abbot Macarius warns the brothers he lives with not to indulge in gossip after attendance at the Eucharist but rather to go away, quietly and reverently, to their cells. Even monks can be distracted from closeness to God by the chance to chat and gossip! The dangers that can short-circuit our connection to God are ever-present and must always be accounted for.

This brings up a very important point: religious life is not only made up of the religious things we do in our lives, it is a matter of how these things work to transform our lives as a whole. All Christians would agree that it is a good thing to say prayers and to go to a service of worship, and Macarius certainly thought it was. What he was try-

---

[58] Ward, Penguin #27, 24

ing to make clear to these monks was that their religious thoughts and religious practice would lose their value if the monks turned immediately to uncharitable actions as soon as they were done. We must use our minds to help direct our whole lives so that it is our religious thoughts and actions that leaven the whole and serve to drive out our faults. We must see our lives whole and govern them according to that broader perspective.

The dangers of distraction do not only lie in the fact that it may interfere with the goods we receive, it can also be the source of difficulties that we might never have faced without it. Another story from the Desert shows this very clearly.[59]

> On a journey a monk met some nuns and when he saw them he turned aside off the road. The abbess said to him, 'If you had been a true monk, you would not have looked to see that we are women.'

In this tale, a monk turns aside from the road so that he will not have to pass close by a party of nuns traveling in the other direction and the Abbess in charge of the nuns tells him that, if he were a real monk, a monk advanced in the religious life, he would have passed them by without any difficulty at all. The difficulty of temptation that he felt at their presence came from within himself, not from them. This monk suffered from a willingness to be distracted away from his primary concern of drawing closer to God. He looked at them to see if they were people who might distract him and, lo and behold, they were! To the person who is looking for ways to be distracted and tempted, almost anything will serve.

---

[59] Ward, Penguin #62, 30

Any Christian, at any time, is subject to this difficulty **as much as he allows himself to be affected by it**. The greatest troubles that afflict our religious lives come from within ourselves and are difficulties we cause ourselves. No amount of going out into the desert, no amount of spending time alone, and no amount of effort can separate us from ourselves. I am convinced that St. Paul's famous statement from his
Letter to the Romans[3]

> "For I am persuaded, that neither death, nor life, nor angels, nor principalities, nor powers, nor things present, nor things to come, Nor height, nor depth, nor any other creature, shall be able to separate us from the love of God, which is in Christ Jesus our Lord."

is meant to be understood with this in mind: only **we** have the power to separate ourselves from the love of God. At some point we must take ourselves in hand and address the difficulties that we cause in our own lives if we are to succeed in making spiritual progress.

The monks of the Desert knew this well, but they also had an overwhelming trust in the power of God's grace and in His desire to offer it to us whenever we need it. They insisted that, if we adhere to God, He will keep us safe and close to Him. For the person who is conscious of God, the strength of God is his strength, the Desert monks taught. That is where the confidence shown in this saying finds its source.[61]

---

[3] 8:38-39
[61] xxiv, 159

> An old man said, "Rising and walking and sitting, if God is before thine eyes, there is naught in which the Enemy can affright thee. If that thought abides in a man, the strength of God shall cleave to him."

Closeness to God makes us more like Him and makes it easier for us to do what we should and to be what we should be. This is why prayer and attention to God are the bedrock of the life of the Christian ascetic.

The stories we have looked at in this chapter have shown us clearly that the Desert Fathers thought that the greatest difficulty in prayer was the difficulty of taming ourselves. Distraction is the greatest enemy to good prayer. This explains why the Fathers insisted so frequently that monks should stay in their cells: it kept them away from distractions, physically, so they would not need to be tested to see if they had the ability to keep themselves away from the distractions that confronted them, mentally and spiritually.

The Desert Fathers are always practical. That can be their greatest lesson to us. If we have difficulty saying our prayers in the living room because of our family, we should go to our bedroom. (Jesus, by the way, tells us in the Sermon on the Mount to do that, anyway, so we should probably have done it before.[62]) If we have difficulty saying prayers in the car or on the bus or the train going to work, we should try to learn to say them at home. If we have difficulty saying them at home, then we should commit them to memory and say them to ourselves as we walk from home to the bus or to the train or as we drive. No one was allowed to enter into the monas-

---

[62] *Matthew* 6:5-6

tic life in the Desert as a member of an organized group until he or she knew enough Psalms to be able to partake in worship from memory. (Since much of their worship centered on the recitation of Psalms, knowing them was a necessary qualification.) The Desert Fathers were convinced that we need to carry around prayer and Scripture in our heads so that we can keep them in our hearts. This was not a requirement designed to keep people out, it was a it was a tool designed to help teach the brothers and sisters freedom from distraction.

One thing that I would like to urge you to do as a part of your attempt to make yourself better able to live a Christian life, is to give yourself the task of committing to memory some of the basic prayers of the Church so that you can pray along with the Church, silently to yourself, without a book and without anyone around you taking notice. There are many times in our lives when this is the only way that we can pray and, if we are not able to pray this way, we will not pray at all. Begin with the collects that are always repeated at Morning and Evening Prayer

---

[63] I refer to The Book of Common Prayer (1928) [see Bibliography], which is a standard presentation of the practice of western Christianity, as influenced by the Reformation. Since the institution of the liturgical changes in the Roman Catholic Communion, the BCP is, in some ways, the most clear representative of the developed western tradition still in use. The services of Morning Prayer and Evening Prayer found in it are simplifications of the daily round of prayer services that had grown more complicated as the history of the Church progressed. Using these services is a way to pray inside the classical Christian tradition in a form that is not overly long or complex. A few days practice will be enough for you to be quite at home with the system. Reading the designated Bible lessons as a part of the services will move you through most of the Scripture over the course of a year.

and with the Canticles that are used in those services.[63] To reduce this teaching to its absolute minimum, every Christian must know the Lord's Prayer by heart and be able to recite that silently to himself as an act of private devotion. If you don't know any Psalms by heart, then you should set yourself the 23rd Psalm to memorize as being the most obvious one with which to begin. With those two things to recite (the Lord's Prayer and the 23rd Psalm), you can begin training yourself to focus on God and your connection to Him. You can do this any time of the day or night; you can do this as often as you remember to do it. The more you pray this way, the more often you will think of doing it and the more your attention will be fixed on God and your relation to Him. This is how the great saints begin. No one should be ashamed of starting from small beginnings.

I heard a story told by an Eastern Orthodox priest of a very holy woman in his parish who clearly had a lively sense of the presence of God and was far advanced in the spiritual life. When he asked her how she prayed, she said, "When I get into bed, I cross myself and fold my hands and say, 'Now I lay me down to sleep…', because that is what my mother taught me." He asked her, "Nothing more?" She answered, "Why say more? That's enough." She was absolutely right, for herself, at least. Some people do not need a lot of words to place themselves in the presence of God. Not everyone may find the same prayer as satisfying as she did, but whatever does the same thing for us as that prayer did for her is enough and appropriate. Remember, **God** is the point, not the words.

Prayer is assumed in all the stories that we inherit from the Desert. We began our look at the Desert monks with it because it is everywhere in their literature, because it is essential, and because it is something we already try to do. If we take no other lesson away for ourselves from the stories from the Desert, at least we should have realized how important putting effort into our Prayer is. The monks of the Desert spent decades on this and were never satisfied, we should at least try to spend a few minutes each day.

Whatsoever things are pure and lovely, whatsoever things are gentle and generous, whatsoever things are noble and self-forgetful, honourable and of good report, these things, O Lord, grant that we may with our whole hearts pursue, through the grace that is given us in Jesus Christ. Amen.[64]

---

[64] Fisher #65, 23

Chapter 8

FASTING AND CHARITY

O Lord, in whose hands are life and death, by whose power we are sustained, forgive us that we have suffered the days and hours of which we must give account to pass away without any endeavour to accomplish thy will. Make us to remember, O God, that every day is thy gift and ought to be used according to thy command. Grant us therefore so to repent of our negligence that we may pass the time which thou shalt yet allow us in diligent service; through Jesus Christ. Amen.[65]

The Desert monks are famous for the severity of their lives. Modern people who know almost nothing about them know that they denied themselves the basic comforts, even the basic necessities, of life for years and years as a part of their search for holiness and closeness to God. When viewed from the outside, however, this Desert practice can easily be misunderstood. Those of us who have not promised to live our lives without eating meat, think of giving up meat as a great deprivation. Those of us who sleep as long as we like, think of giving up hours of sleep each night as a great deprivation. Those of us who are easily bored by any repetition in our lives, think of the prospect of living a life according to a set rule as

---

[65] Fisher #62, 22 (a prayer of Samuel Johnson)

the worst kind of prison, but these are not the views of the people inside the Desert Tradition.

To begin with, asceticism was never an end in itself with the Desert monks. It was, instead, a carefully-thought-out means of organizing their lives and focusing their attention on the things that they had decided were the most important and most useful for ordering their lives toward attention to God. Desert monks were ferocious ascetics, but they did not love fasting for its own sake, and they did not think that it was more important than it is. Here is a story about the struggle against lust that will begin to show us a bit of what they thought fasting could do for them.[66]

> A certain brother questioned an old man about imaginings of this kind. And the old man said to him, "I myself have never been goaded by this thing." And the brother was scandalized at him and went off to another old man saying, "Behold, this is what the old man said to me, and I was scandalized at him: for what he says is beyond nature." And the old man said, "Not in foolishness was this said to thee by the man of God: arise and go, and do penance before him, that he may open to thee the wisdom in his words." So the brother rose up and came to the old man, and did penance in his sight. And he said, "Forgive me, Father, in that I behaved like a fool, and left thee without bidding thee farewell: but I entreat thee to explain to me how

---

[66] xxxi, 85-86

thou hast never been harried by lust." The old man said to him, "Since that time that I became a monk I have never given myself my fill of bread, nor of water, nor of sleep, and tormenting myself with appetite for these things whereby we are fed, I was not suffered to feel the stings of lust". And the brother went away, profiting by the old man's tale.

The role fasting plays in this story is absolutely clear. It is not something that has value in itself, but is rather something that is a means to an end, a tool to achieve a goal that is valuable apart from the fast. Fasting is, therefore, a part of the Christian life because preparation for virtue is an important element in the Christian life, but fasting is not the goal of the Christian life and it is not the highest element in the Christian life.

Since modern people tend to be suspicious of early monks, assuming that they were grim individuals, I would like to show you that this understanding of the story we just read is not my own but rather is that of the tradition itself. I do not want you to think that I am making the Desert literature more "modern" to make it more appealing. Look at this story, which is clear on the limit of the value of fasting and is also meant as a joke. The Desert was harsh, but some of them kept a sense of humor.[67]

A brother asked a certain old man, saying, "There be two brothers, and one of them is quiet in his cell, and prolongs his fast for

---

[67] xviii, 129

six days, and lays much travail on himself:
but the other tends the sick. Whose work is
the more acceptable to God?" And the old
man answered, "If that brother who carries
his fast for six days were to hang himself up
by the nostrils, he could not equal the other,
who does service to the sick."

The contrast in value between charitable works and
asceticism, which, even if it works, helps only the person
who practices it, is **no comparison at all**. The Desert
tradition values charitable work and concern for others
over even the most extreme ascetical practices. Asceticism
is not valuable in and of itself, in the eyes of the monks
of the Desert. If we put that part of their lives in the
forefront of our minds when we think about them, we
distort our picture of what they were trying to do and
risk making them out to have been a very different group
than they really were.

Let's look at another story on this topic: a charming
one, and attractive to me because I'm a great admirer of
Epiphanius the bishop of Cyprus who appears in it. It
teaches much the same lesson.[68]

At one time Epiphanius bishop of Cyprus
sent to the Abbot Hilarion, asking him and
saying, "Come that I may see thee, before I
go forth from the body. "And when they had
come together, and were eating, a portion of
fowl was brought them: and the bishop took
it and gave it to the abbot Hilarion. And the

---

[68] xv, 76

old man said to him, "Forgive me, Father, but from the time that I took this habit, I have eaten naught that hath been killed." And Epiphanius said to him "And I from the time that I took this habit have let no man sleep that had aught against me, nor have I slept holding aught against any man." And the old man said to him, "Forgive me, for thy way of life is greater than mine."

The Desert tradition, in fact, includes quite a number of stories that sound like tales celebrating abstinence but turn out to be, instead, stories told in praise of charity. Since the tradition of the Desert is to teach through the telling of stories, I don't feel too bad for not being able to resist giving you the last paragraph of a set of stories about the Holy Macarius:[69]

They tell that once a certain brother brought a bunch of grapes to the holy Macarius: but he who for love's sake thought not on his own things but on the things of others, carried it to another brother, who seemed more feeble. And the sick man gave thanks to God for the kindness of his brother, but he too thinking more of his neighbor than of himself, brought it to another, and he again to another, and so that same bunch of grapes was carried around all the cells, scattered as they were far over the desert, and no one knowing who first had sent it, it was brought

---

[69] 61-62

last to the first giver. But the Holy Macarius gave thanks that he had seen in the brethren such abstinence and such loving-kindness and did himself reach after still sterner discipline of the life of the spirit.

Isn't that a wonderful story of the sublime absurdity of a whole group of monks trying to act in perfect charity and so having the problem of there being no one among them who could resist the urge to be charitable long enough to enjoy the gift that had been given him? It seems that the grapes were never eaten at all, unless they were given to some visitor from the outside who would be bound by the code of hospitality to eat what was set before him. This, also, is a joke that points out the result of having a whole group of people who were really (for a time, at least) living up to the teaching of *Philippians* 2:3-4:

> Let nothing be done through strife or vainglory; but in lowliness of mind let each esteem other better than themselves.
> Look not every man on his own things, but every man also on the things of others.

Here again, in this comic story, we are shown the supreme importance of care for others and the unworldly heights we can attain if we really pursue it.

This glimpse into the life of the Desert that the last story presents us is valuable and instructive for our understanding of how their lives really worked. We see that there were a relatively large number of monks living individually in separate cells in the same vicinity. This allowed solitude as well as visiting back-and-forth and communal worship. We also see that they knew enough about each other to have some idea about how the other monks were doing, physically and spiritually. That helps explain the practical charity described in the story and also reminds us of the general tendency among monks of the Desert to visit each other, asking for instructions and, sometimes, offering instruction. But what does the story tell us about fasting?

The renouncing of sleep, food, sex, and companionship by the monk was meant to force him to engage actively in living a Christian life. So much talk and effort has always been spent on fasting among the religious because of the weakness of Christians, not because of their fortitude. This is a very important point.

The Christian tradition speaks about fasting over and over again, not because Christians are good at fasting and not because Christians fast all the time, but because, in order to get them to do even a little bit of fasting to help them focus their lives, great emphasis and repetition is necessary. Anyone who has ever worked as a schoolteacher or anyone who has ever acted as a parent to children knows exactly why this is necessary. It is not always the most important things that are the most stressed by those in authority. (Where is the parent who thinks that chewing with one's mouth shut is the most important trait of an adult in this life? But where is the parent who does not spend a good 20% of his energy on that topic? At times, I feel that I have never talked about anything else! My children report that they feel the same way.) It is, rather, the things that the people being instructed are the least willing or able to do that are stressed. Presumably, the greatest saint would not need to fast at all, but would proceed directly to living the Christian life, leaving the preparations for that process behind.

Fasting of various kinds is a good and useful tool in the Christian life. Any Christian who has ever taken part in a "quiet day" at church is, himself, fasting from idle conversation to help himself focus on things that are more useful. Any Christian who rouses himself to pray, even though he is exhausted, is fasting as well as praying, because he is giving up sleep. "Fasting", properly understood, is the ordering of our lives in a way that will better support our Christian devotion and understanding. The monks of the Desert did not fast more than we do because they valued fasting more, but because they valued Christian living more and hated sinfulness more than we do. Their fasting was a sign of their realization that they were their own biggest stumbling blocks on the path to righteousness. If we are faithful imitators of the Desert monks, we will not necessarily give up food and sleep but will turn our minds and hearts to examining **honestly** how we measure up to our ideals and will take real steps to see that we make progress toward that goal.

Asceticism is no grounds for pride and no prize in itself, any more than time spent on playing scales on an instrument is making music. The music comes in the concert and the righteousness is found in the actual living of a Christian life. A sandwich given to a hungry person or a lunch shared with a friend who forgot to bring one is a greater act of virtue than any abstemious Lent, in the eyes of the Desert Fathers. Wasn't this also the teaching of Jesus in the parable of the Good Samaritan? The

Desert tradition is doing nothing other than showing us the Gospel in new clothing.

> Grant us, O Lord, not to mind earthly things, but to love things heavenly; and even now, while we are placed among things that are passing away, to cleave to those that shall abide; through Jesus Christ our Lord. Amen.[70]

---

[70] Fisher #55, 21 (from the Leonine Sacramentary, 440 AD)

Chapter 9

LIVING WITH THE SINFUL URGES IN US

> O Lamb of God that takest away the sins of the world,
> Have mercy upon us.
> O Lamb of God that takest away the sins of the world,
> Have mercy upon us.
> O Lamb of God that takest away the sins of the world,
> Grant us thy peace.

One of the things that seems to separate those who actually engage in an attempt to lead a religious Christian life from those who look at such attempts from the outside is that outsiders tend to romanticize Christian asceticism. We see them in their picturesque habits, we think of them living in the Forest or in the Desert, praying long and wrestling with demons and it seems like an heroic and wonderful thing to do. I have a friend who has been a Trappist monk for more than 50 years now and he tells me that monks do not romanticize their own lives because they know how difficult they are and how unremitting the problems are. There is a strong strain of this realization of the difficulty of serious Christian living in the stories that come down to us from the Egyptian desert. Here is a good example of that practical teaching.[71]

---

[71] Ward, Penguin #15, 91-92

They said of one hermit that for fifty years he ate no bread and drank very little water. He said, 'I have destroyed lust and greed and vanity.' When Abraham heard that he had said this, he came to him and said, 'Was it you who said this?' He answered, 'Yes.' Abraham said to him, 'Supposing you go into your cell and find a woman on your mat, could you think she was not a woman?' He said, 'No. But I would fight against my thoughts, so as not to touch her.' Abraham said, 'Then you have not killed lust, the passion is still alive; you have only imprisoned it. Suppose you were walking along a road and saw stones on one side and gold in jars on the other, could you think the gold and the stones were of the same value?' her answered, 'No, but I would resist my desire and not let myself pick it up.' Abraham said to him, 'Then the passion still lives, you have only imprisoned it.' He went on, 'If you heard that one brother loved you and spoke well of you, and another brother hated you and slandered you, and they both came to visit you, would they both be equally welcome to you?' He said, 'No: but I would force myself to treat him who hates me just as well as him who loves me.' So Abraham said to him, 'Then your passions are alive, only in some measure holy men have got them chained.'

This story, and the repetition in it of different temptations that are suggested by Abba Abraham, shows very clearly the on-going and repeated nature of the failures of serious Christians to be perfect. This comes straight from the heart of the New Testament. It is a **dogma** of the Christian tradition, that is, it is taken as an absolute **fact** by the Christian tradition, that all human beings sin.[72]

> "For all have sinned, and come short of the glory of God;"

All of us know that, from experience, if not from reading it in Scripture or being taught it in a sermon or class, but it is important to see that the Desert tradition acknowledges this openly and faces it squarely. How else could it possibly help those who want real, useful advice? The Desert monks were real people trying to live real Christian lives; they were not figments of our imagination or characters in a play. They had to look at their lives honestly or they could not have any hope of finding their way through the maze that this world can be for those who are seeking God and godliness. We can never see the Desert tradition clearly if we do not realize that it was the product of many thousands of Christians living serious lives in pursuit of closeness to God. They did not want other people to think they were serious Christians, they wanted to **be** serious Christians. That is a real desire of real people for their lives in the "real world". What this sense of reality means is that the Desert tradition describes Christian life as it is actually lived, not in an abstract and ideal form.

Now, there are three possible responses to the realization that we will never be perfect.

- We might despair and think that all attempts at

---

[72] *Romans* 3:23

being good Christians are pointless because we can never be perfect.

- Second, we might decide that the idea of "being good" is meaningless. (We can never be perfectly good, so therefore, "good" and "evil" are useless categories and would better be discarded. Many people talk this way in public in our society today, but this is not a new idea and I have no reason to think it is actually more widely spread now than ever before. However, it certainly is loudly fashionable, now, in a way that is unusual in history.)

- Third, we can rededicate ourselves to the task of being as good as we can. We can focus our efforts and energy on paying attention to God and drawing closer to God, despite the fact that we know that we will never reach Him and that we can never be worthy of Him. This is the response of the Desert tradition.

Let me offer you some examples of how it teaches us to confront this difficulty. Before we look at them, however, it is important for you to recognize that these do not offer what we might call "solutions" to this problem. This is not because I am hiding their solution from you or because they were hiding it from all of us. The Desert tradition taught what it had discovered: there are some things that we are able only to battle against but not to overcome. The stories we will look at reflect the fruit of their experience. These stories are exciting because they offer us a real sense of what the Desert dwellers experienced and how they tried to meet and overcome it in their pursuit of progress in Christian living.[73]

---

[73] xxii, 76

One of the brethren asked the abbot Isidore, an old man in Scete[74], saying, "Wherefore do the devils fear thee so mightily?" And the old man said to him, "From the time that I was made a monk, I have striven not to suffer anger to mount as far as my throat."

It is interesting to see that the struggles of living a religious life showed the monks the reasonable bounds of what they could expect to achieve. Abba Isidore does not seem to consider the possibility of living a life in which anger never arises in him, but he does attempt to govern his anger and stop it from controlling him. He is talking about the **management of sinfulness**, not its eradication. The monk who listens to this story is not presented with the hope of escaping from the temptations that come upon us in this world, but is offered the example of a man who has seriously tried to tame his sinfulness. This is not a romantic view of monks achieving perfect and blissful sinlessness, but a realistic acknowledgement of the grittiness of living out the Christian life as a sinful person in a wicked world.

This next story addresses the fact that temptations can come to us, not only in the present, but also from the past. People who have physically removed themselves from certain temptations are often surprised to discover that the temptations continue to live in their heads and accompany them wherever they go. This story addresses that very discouraging trial of the serious Christian.[75]

A hermit asked a brother, 'Do you often talk with women?' the brother said, 'No.' He

---

[74] Scete (pronounced "skeet") was one of the main settlements of the Desert monks. (author's note)
[75] Ward, Penguin #6, 35

went on, 'My temptations come from paint-
ings old and new, memories of mine which
trouble me through pictures of women.' But
the hermit said to him, 'Do not fear the dead,
but flee the living; flee from consenting to
sin or committing sin, and take a longer time
over your prayers.'

The old man does not promise that these tempting
memories will some day disappear, instead, he turns the
attention of the brother to how he will **respond** to these
distractions. What matters in the spiritual life is not so
much the encounters we have with temptations, for all
people experience them, whether in the flesh or in our
minds, but, rather, our response to them. "Take a longer
time over your prayers" is a teaching designed to return
the brother's attention to God, which would automatically, therefore, prevent him from dwelling on his dis-
tracting memories. It is a teaching that can be followed
every time one finds himself in need of renewing his focus on God, so it is a teaching that expects to be followed
not once, but over and over again.

The prominence of stories of fasting in the records
from the Desert shows that the problem of temptations
arising within them never went away for the monks, just
as it never does for us. (After all, if they had conquered
these inner demons, they could have given up their fasts.)
What defined the monks as a group was how seriously
they tried to fight the fight against temptation, not the
fact that they ever won that battle. The lesson they teach
us is one of moral seriousness and maturity. Only the
truly mature, the spiritually mature, can live with failure
without giving in to despair or offering to surrender.

How can we do this? How can we persevere when we are not succeeding? The Desert Fathers did it by instructing each other in ways to approach fighting temptation and by constant, never failing encouragement of each other in the face of their short-comings. This is one of the areas in which the community in the Desert was the most active and, perhaps, the most important. For us, as we look for ways to apply the lessons of the Desert to our daily lives, I think this strain of thought shows us two ways to confront this challenge of the constant presence of temptation in our lives.

First, it shows us that we should not expect complete success in our battle with temptation and that we can, in fact, never achieve it in this life.

It also shows us that we can draw on each other for encouragement in the difficult moments of our religious lives. Sometimes, just seeing the other faces at weekly worship is enough to remind us of the fact that, though each of us fights alone, we fight as individual soldiers in the same army. Sometimes we need something more tangible and individual than that, however, and we turn to friends and books and clergy for help.

The Fathers and Mothers of the Desert did this, too. They visited each other and asked for counsel, they read books of spiritual advice and read Scripture, hoping for enlightenment and strength, and they turned to the priests among them and the nearby bishops for information and solace. It is clear that this is the element in the religious experience in the Desert that sparked the creation of the writings that survive for us to read.

The Desert monks wrote down the advice of their elders in Christ so that others coming after them could benefit from the spiritual wisdom of the people whom they, themselves, turned to. When we pick up a volume of the Desert Fathers' writings and read it, we are not only entering into a relationship with that tradition, we are also acting in the way that the members of that tradition acted. There is no more traditional Desert practice than turning to a book of the writings of the Desert Fathers for help in time of need. When you pick up this volume and read these chapters, you form a part of the longest ongoing tradition of spiritual encouragement and counsel the Christian Church can offer. It is a great treasure to have and a great challenge to us, if we allow it to confront us. If we appreciate it fully, we will be both comforted and spurred on by it to continue making efforts to heighten our religious lives. If we listen to its teaching, our failures will never lead us to despair.

> Watch thou, dear Lord, with those who wake, or watch, or weep tonight, and give thine angels charge over those who sleep. Tend thy sick ones, O Lord Christ; rest thy weary ones; bless thy dying ones. Soothe thy suffering ones; shield thy joyous ones; and all for thy Love's sake. Amen.[76]

---

[76] Fisher #221, 77 (a prayer of St. Augustine)

Chapter 10

SERMON AT SUNDAY SERVICE
Sermon text: *Luke* 18:9-14

And he spake this parable unto certain
which trusted in themselves that they
were righteous, and despised others:
Two men went up into the temple to
pray; the one a Pharisee, and the other a
publican.
The Pharisee stood and prayed thus
with himself, God, I thank thee, that I
am not as other men are, extortioners,
unjust, adulterers, or even as this
publican.
I fast twice in the week, I give tithes of
all that I possess.
And the publican, standing afar off,
would not lift up so much as his eyes
unto heaven, but smote upon his breast,
saying, God be merciful to me a sinner.
I tell you, this man went down to his
house justified rather than the other: for
every one that exalteth himself shall be
abased; and he that humbleth himself
shall be exalted.

It is unusual for a gospel to begin a parable with a
line that serves to guide its interpretation. The fact that
St. Luke has chosen to include this introduction in his

recitation of this parable is interesting for us and instructive. It shows clearly what St. Luke wanted to teach his audience when he included the story in his gospel, but it does not excuse us from the need to make sense of what this story shows us that is relevant to our own lives. I think this short parable contains two separate lessons for us to take to heart.

It seems clear, both from the New Testament tradition and from the content of the Gospel, that St. Luke's Gospel was intended to address the Gentile portion of the Church. Because of this, it is reasonable to think that St. Luke would be concerned that his audience might have concluded that this parable makes a contrast between the wicked Jewish religious authorities and the spiritually good people of whom the Jews disapproved. In other words, they might hear this story as describing **them** (Gentile Christians) as a group enjoying God's particular favor and the Jewish part of the Church, especially those who were particularly attached to traditional Jewish practice, as being less favored by God.

The New Testament makes perfectly clear that, for a large portion of the Jewish Christians in the first generation of the Church, the Gentiles were second class members of the Church, at best. It is important for us to realize, however, that it may well have been the case that the Gentile members thought the Jewish members were less than ideal, too. After all (the Gentile Christians might tell themselves) it was some of the Jewish religious authorities who arranged the death of Jesus. Throughout Christian history, less thoughtful and less discerning Christians have periodically tended to confuse the particular individuals shown in the Gospel scenes with the entire group from which they were drawn. This is a great evil and a great misunderstanding, but I do not wish to speak about it now. I mention it because I think it should remind us that the New Testament was shaped, both by its Divine Author and by its human authors, with the Church's needs at that time as well as with thoughts of its future in mind. The Holy Ghost, through the pen of Luke, offers us in the first line of this parable, a declaration that this teaching is not one that is historically bound to the particular time and place in which an encounter like this could have happened (that is, the Temple in Jerusalem) but rather is one that has a universally applicable, spiritual message. In other words, I would like the first point I make to be that the introduction to this parable offered by St. Luke shows both the sinful tendency of members of the Church at all times, as well as God's desire to lead us through that sinfulness to a better understanding of Him and to a better life.

The second point of this parable is the central one. Two people stand in the presence of God. One of them is a scrupulous and pious fulfiller of religious duty. There is no reason to think of him as hypocritical and no reason to think of him as dishonest. He stands in the parable as a representative of the man who is focused on fulfilling his religious obligations. Next to him stands a man who has chosen a life that makes normal religious activity impossible. As a tax collector, he must spend much of his time in contact with ritually unclean Gentiles. As a tax collector, his work supports a Gentile regime that rules over the People of God without any respect for its special religious character. As a tax collector, he has placed himself outside the bounds of normal Jewish life. Still, he is not completely divorced from the Jewish religious tradition. When he presents himself at the Temple and addresses

God, it is with a highly developed sense of where his life has led him and what that means for his connection to God. (That is, he is fully and honestly aware of his sinfulness.) This is the contrast that our Lord wants us to take to heart. The questions to ask ourselves are, "How do people relate to God?" and "Where do these two people find themselves located along the possible spectrum in that broader relationship?".

The teaching of the Bible is clear that all human beings are unworthy of the presence and love of God.[77] God loves us anyway, while we are still unworthy, as St. John says,[78] but our unworthiness remains. It is a part of the fallen nature we inherit and a sad truth about the fallen world in which we live. One of the pair in this parable, the Pharisee, has spent his life trying to be worthy of God. Because he has tried to achieve worthiness, he mistakenly thinks that he has made himself actually worthy. This is his great error.

The other man has not done as he should have done, and yet, when he approaches God's presence in the Temple, **he** is the one who knows his true religious position and what it means. The Pharisee in this story has the right to be glad that he has successfully fulfilled his religious duties (a right the Publican does not share), but his understanding of the **meaning** of that is completely false and renders his fulfillment of those duties void of value, as a consequence. This story illustrates one of the great pitfalls awaiting those who are lucky enough to be conscientious about their relationship with God.

---

[77] *Romans* 3:23
[78] *1 John* 4:9-10

All of us owe a duty to God. We owe him more than we can ever repay. It is not enough to say that we owe Him everything we have, for we owe Him existence itself. The Pharisee's life has been spent appropriately, because it has been spent in activities that make this debt obvious and lead to a recognition of the true relationship between the human being and the Divine. The failure he falls into is a characteristic failure of the religious person: he thinks that, because he has behaved in ways that show a realization of the gulf between his nature and God's, he has therefore fulfilled his obligation. This is where he steps over the bounds of piety straight into blasphemy.

The tax collector who stands next to him has wasted his life, as far as religious duty is concerned. Still, like a hedgehog, he knows one great thing, and that is that he is unworthy of the presence and favor of God.

We are confronted in this story, then, with a good life and a misspent life, but the good life has led the person who has engaged in it **away** from God and the misspent life has led the person who has engaged in it **toward** God. Since both have been unable to attain to God and be worthy of God, who is better off as they stand in His presence? It is, ironically, the tax collector.

The lesson of this parable, then, falls into line very neatly with one of the main thrusts of the teaching of Jesus during His ministry: what matters most to God is not the particular history of our lives, but rather our ability to understand where we are in our relationship to God and what we need to do next to improve it. It has always been difficult for upright, pious people to take this teaching of Jesus to heart. It seems unfair and unjust that sinful people should be given the same chance of closeness to

God as those who have spent difficult and taxing lives in His service, but such is the teaching of our Lord.

Christianity is a demanding Faith. In this regard, it mirrors the demanding nature of the world in which we live. Effort, by itself, is not rewarded in this life, and attaining the Kingdom of Heaven seems to work the same way. No matter how hard we try to walk home, if we don't know in what direction to begin, we are likely to take ourselves **farther** from our goal, not nearer. Effort without knowledge can be worse than useless, because it can leave us farther from our goal than we began. This seems to have been the case with the Pharisee. It is likely that he began his religious life because he sensed that he needed to draw closer to God. In this, he was absolutely correct. However, the result of this effort was not that he drew closer to God. Rather, his effort was the cause of him losing his grasp on the insight that had impelled him to pursue it in the beginning. He was worse off than when he began. For us, I think, this is the great lesson in this parable.

The Gospel offers us Grace that will draw us to God and make us acceptable to Him. This is the only way that we can reach Him. It is a characteristic of fallen human nature that the very same sense of distance between us and God can also serve to prevent us from moving over that distance toward God, because, once we have begun to acknowledge that separation, we begin to congratulate ourselves for our piety and good sense, and so end by admiring our own goodness instead of focusing on the gulf that remains between us and God! How ironic it is, that this same religious desire that should make us open to God can be the very thing that cuts us off from Him, if we fail in our understanding of our true nature and

His! Our Lord, because He saw into the hearts of men, realized this danger and this short parable points it out to us, directly.

Here we are, gathered together, in an unreligious age, as a group of people who are very conscious of religious truths. How tragic and ironic it would be if we allowed that very awareness to **keep** us from the presence of God rather than to draw us to Him! If we ever slip and begin to think of ourselves as specially chosen or especially worthy, then we will have failed, indeed. We will have allowed our great blessing to become a burden to us and an obstacle in our path to God.

This was the great tragedy of the Pharisee in the Temple. The honesty and piety in him that began him on the path to God ended by rising up in his mind as **his own virtue**, instead of his realizing it as a sign of God's Grace being active in him, and he ended by glorying in himself instead of in God's graciousness. This tendency to attribute our blessings to ourselves instead of the God Who gives them to us is what St. Paul warns of in *1 Corinthians*:[79]

> But God hath chosen the foolish things
> of the world to confound the wise; and
> God hath chosen the weak things of the
> world to confound the things which are
> mighty;
> And base things of the world, and things
> which are despised, hath
> God chosen, yea, and things which are

---

[79] 1:27-31

not, to bring to nought things that are:
That no flesh should glory in his presence.
But of him are ye in Christ Jesus, who
of God is made unto us wisdom, and
righteousness, and sanctification, and
redemption:
That, according as it is written, He that
glorieth, let him glory in the Lord.

The Psalmist, at the start of Psalm 115, states the proper attitude for creatures to have toward their Creator as clearly as we ever see it in the Bible:[80]

Not unto us, O LORD, not unto us,
but unto thy name give glory, for thy
mercy, and for thy truth's sake.

Experiencing the grace of God is an intoxicating thing, but we must try to keep our heads, nevertheless. The grace of God is so all encompassing that even those of us who are tax collectors can hope to be drawn to Him, purely through His response to our own admission of our own unworthiness. Let us never lose the clear sense of God's majesty and holiness that will always remind us of our own unworthiness of Him and unlikeness to Him. That sense of God's majesty is what can guard us from this Pharisaical failing of self-satisfaction. That sense of God's holiness is what can keep our eyes firmly fixed on our goal. That sense in us of God's holiness and majesty is what will let His grace draw us close to Him in the end, if only we can keep our eyes on **Him** instead of on ourselves.

---

[80] 115:1

Chapter 11

SPIRITUAL PRIDE

O God, who scatterest the proud in the imagination of their hearts, forgive us our sins of pride, especially our pride in our own worth in Thy sight. May we never despise our fellow men, but make each of us, in honour, prefer the other, for Jesus Christ's sake. Amen.[81]

The great temptation of the serious Christian is to fall into spiritual pride. Because few Christians in the history of the Church have been more serious than the men and women living in the desert of Egypt in the 300s and 400s, they were particularly liable to this temptation. Because they were so serious about their religious lives, however, they were well aware of this pitfall and spoke and thought and wrote much about it. It is one of the most constantly discussed difficulties in all the collections of Desert literature. Because of this, we should take the time to examine this topic. It is characteristic of the Desert movement and an important strand in its teaching. There is, however, a more practical and immediate reason for us looking at this teaching, as well.

All of us involved in this process, from me who thinks it worthwhile to write this book to all of you who are still

---

[81] Fisher #28, 14 (altered). See *Philippians* 2:3-4 for one place this prayer echoes. Those verses can rightly be called the kernel of Christian teaching about ethical behavior.

bothering to read it, are surely displaying more serious religious interests than many people do. In a society that is not very seriously inclined to religion, though it is certainly superficially interested in religion, we can rightly describe ourselves as people who take religion seriously. This is a great blessing, but also a great challenge. The temptations that confronted the Desert Fathers confront us, also. It is very easy for us to pat ourselves on the back and congratulate ourselves for our spiritual maturity and seriousness, but this would be a grave mistake. If we fall into the trap of regarding ourselves as spiritually advanced and adept, we will be falling into the snare that the Desert Fathers knew of and worried about. Over the next few pages, as we look at some of the teachings of the Desert Fathers on spiritual pride, we should not listen to them as speaking of other people's difficulties, in other times and places, but, rather, we should take them very seriously to heart as warnings and challenges for us, here and now. If we engage ourselves in this study only to blind ourselves to our own inadequacies, how is our effort benefiting us? If we take ourselves off on our own to reflect on religious matters only to congratulate ourselves on our holiness and worthiness, how do we benefit from that thinking? Let us see what the Desert Fathers said.[82]

> There was a certain one that abstained from food and ate no bread: he came to one of the Fathers. By chance there came also other pilgrims, and the old man made them a little broth. And when they sat down to eat,

---

[82] xxii, 100-101

the abstemious brother set down for himself a pea that he had steeped, and chewed it. And when they got up from table, the old man took him aside and said to him, "Brother, if thou comest to anyone, do not show off to him thy way of life: if thou dost wish to keep to thine own way, abide in thy cell and go nowhere out from it." And he accepted the words of the old man, and made himself thereafter share the common life in whatsoever fell to his lot with the brethren.

You notice that the old man does not condemn the way of life of the abstemious brother. We are not meant to think that there is anything wrong with the way the brother is living. The brother goes off track when he thinks his way of life makes him special. He sins through his joy in showing that specialness off to those around him (and to himself) when he mixes with them. This is his way of being spiritually proud: he considers himself more devout than others and delights in it.

There is a charming story about the same difficulty[83] that shows some of the monks making a visit to the hermits of the deep desert, not to gain wisdom from them but to compare themselves to them to see if their own manner of life was superior to those famous ascetics. This story is worth repeating at length because it shows so many of the characteristics of Desert teaching, both in content and in manner.

---

[83] Ward, Wisdom #97, 31-32

Some brothers from a monastery went to the desert to visit an anchorite who received them with joy. According to the custom amongst hermits, when he saw their fatigue, he set the table before the usual time and brought what he had to refresh them. When evening came, they recited the twelve Psalms, and likewise during the night. While he was keeping vigil all alone, he heard them saying amongst themselves, 'The anchorites in the desert have a softer life than we do in the monastery'. At early dawn while they were preparing to leave and to visit the neighbouring old man, he said to them, 'Greet him from me and say to him, "Do not water the vegetables".' This they did. When he heard these words, the other old man understood what it meant, and he kept them at work until evening. When evening came, he recited the great *synaxis* and said, 'Let us stop now, for your sakes, for you are tired', and he went on, 'It is not our custom to eat every day, but for your sakes let us eat a little.' He brought them dry bread and salt saying, 'For your sake we must celebrate', and he poured a little vinegar on the salt. When they rose from the table, they said the *synaxis* till early dawn. Then he said to them, 'We cannot fulfil the whole rule on your account; you must take a little rest, for you come from far.' When morning came, they wanted to escape, but he begged them saying, 'Stay yet awhile with us, at least three days according to the commandment, so as to follow the traditional custom of the desert.' But seeing that he would not send them away, they arose and escaped secretly.

The story ends with the visitors sneaking away in the night in order to escape the tough lives of the hermits. They were humbled and could no longer think of themselves as special, which was what the hermits had hoped to make them feel. The hermits in this story are fulfilling one of their primary roles: to teach their fellows by example, while the visiting monks have stepped outside the true Desert tradition by hoping to feel triumphant on account of their own virtue. This sort of competition is antithetical to the Desert's focus on self-reproach and constant awareness of one's own sinfulness. If you are really reflecting on your own sins, your only thought regarding your brothers and sisters would be to pray for them to be freed from their sins so they do not have to suffer from them as you do from yours. Any kind of comparison between yourself and them, especially to your own advantage, would never come to your mind.

Nowadays, we tend not to compete with each other over fasting, but we do compete. Every group of people has its own areas of competition. The particular bone of contention is not important, what matters is the reason we want to compete. The desire to think of ourselves as special and to glory in our own virtue is what the Desert tradition was thinking of when it told these stories. **That** tendency lurks in **all** human breasts, I am convinced. All of us can see ourselves in that abstemious brother who ate only one pea and in those brothers who visited the hermits of the deep desert and can feel ourselves rebuked.

Paul S. Russell

It is important to see that the Desert monks were not only concerned that our relations with other people might spur us to spiritual pride, they also were concerned that we might stray in this direction even when we are not interacting with anyone else. Along these lines, the monks told another story[84] that shows that the human tendency to self-congratulation can find food to feed on even when we are alone.

> It was said that a hermit was working earnestly in his cell, wrapped up in his mat. He went to visit Ammon, who saw him using his mat like this, and said to him, 'That is not a good idea.' The hermit said, 'Three thoughts trouble me. The first is that I ought to go and live somewhere else in the desert; the second is that I should go out and find a foreign country where no one knows me; the third is that I should shut myself in my cell, see no one, and eat every other day.' Ammon said to him, 'None of these three would be any use to you. Stay in your cell, eat a little every day, always keep in your heart the words of the publican in the Gospel, and you can be saved (Luke 18:13).'

This monk is always trying to do more than he has been doing. He sees no limit to his ability to undergo hardship in his pursuit of perfection and goes to see Ammon with three suggestions for increasing his austerity,

---

[84] Ward, Penguin #16, 92. Notice that Abba Ammon refers him to the same gospel lesson that we used in the last chapter. Christian teaching on this point is very consistent.

each more severe than the last. Ammon's reply brings him down to earth with a bump. It is not our ability to do difficult things that matters and sitting in our cell (usually a mark of great self-denial and seriousness for a Desert monk) is of no use if we spend our time there thinking about our sanctity. What matters is the content of our heart, teaches Ammon. The clear-eyed self-reproach of the Publican in *Luke* 18, who would not lift his eyes to heaven and knew his own sins, is the goal of the monk. For this monk, austerity had become a self-defeating trap and Ammon directed him away from it to the real heart of the matter: our spiritual disposition. One of the things this makes clear is how much the Desert monks learned about human psychology in the course of their efforts to better themselves. We are so prone to pride that we can sin for no better reason than to show off to ourselves!

If pride is such a common human fault, even an inescapable fault, how are we to avoid it? The Desert tradition likes to teach people by giving them examples to follow rather than by giving them abstract principles. This is something that the broader Christian tradition has also favored. The universal tradition in the Church of remembering, recording and recounting the lives of saints works on the same principle. (Protestants practice this as much as any other Christians, as a visit to any Evangelical bookstore will show you, where shelves are filled with lives of Calvin and Luther and Whitefield and Wesley as well as many biographies of great missionaries: Protestant saints for Protestant devotion. Think of Foxe's *Book of Christian Martyrs*, too, which is, by far, the most famous example

---

[85] If you have never read any of these, I urge you to do so. If you have already read some of these, I urge you to read the lives of saints from before the division of the Church into Protestant and Catholic and from beyond the bounds of the western branch of

of this sort of devotion in the English speaking part of the Protestant stream in Christian history.[85])

There has been a great deal of scholarly work done on the Desert tradition in recent decades and one of the things people have noticed is that the monks of the Desert tended to read Scripture in search of spiritual examples, in much the same way as they read writings from their own tradition. The monks were looking for examples of holiness to follow so they liked to find saints' lives in the Bible, too. This story shows us an example of that in action:[86]

> The abbot Mathois said, "The nearer a man approaches to God, the greater sinner he sees himself to be. For the prophet Isaiah saw God, and said that he was unclean and undone."

One of the things we see here is that the monks looked on the characters in Scripture as their spiritual forbears. Another thing we see is that they believed that progress in the spiritual life brings with it a diminishment of spiritual pride. I think if we look at the history of the Church we can see that this is, in fact, correct. Certainly, one of the characteristics that saints such as Francis of Assisi,

the Christian tree. We can all learn much from spending time reflecting on the holy lives lived by other Christians gone before us. Christians from more catholic backgrounds will be amazed at how Catholic the Protestant saints seem and Protestants will be amazed at how Evangelical the Catholic saints seem. Nothing is more ecumenical than sanctity.

[86] xxviii, 124. Abba Mathois is referring to *Isaiah* 6:1-13 when Isaiah sees the Lord in the Temple.

Therese of Lisieux and Thomas á Becket (not to mention John Wesley and Jonathan Edwards) shared in common is that they all seem to have had a very lively sense of their sinfulness, while those around them were convinced of their great sanctity. This sense of not being better than anyone else seems to be an integral element in what the Church has always recognized as holiness. It is interesting to see that the Desert monks thought of this quality in the same way. We can see this conviction illustrated in the following story:[87]

> The old men said that once certain folk had given the brethren in Scete a few dried figs, and because they were paltry they sent none of them to the abbot Arsenius, lest he might feel himself insulted. But when he heard of it, he did not go out as usual to the celebration of the holy office with the brethren, saying, "Ye have excommunicated me, in that ye would not give me the present that the Lord sent to the brethren, because I was not worthy to receive it." And when they all heard it, they were moved by the humility of the old man, and the priest set out and took him some of the dried figs and brought him back happy to the congregation.

That is a useful story to consider as we try to bring together these different insights into a clear picture of what the Desert Fathers considered was an appropriate way of thinking about oneself. Clearly, they understood spiri-

---

[87] viii, 122

tual pride to be something that arises in the heart of the individual Christian. This is why their stories describe it as being a sin that can come upon us when we examine others and find them not up to our standards, a sin that can attack us when we are alone and reflect on our own particular wonderfulness, or a sin that can come upon us when we spend time in community. In other words, they suggest no way to order our lives that will not allow this sin to arise.

Since the difficulty lies within ourselves, it is within ourselves that it must be attacked and conquered. There is no way to avoid occasions that will allow it, because the pride of the human heart is such that any occasion will allow it to take over. What the serious Christian should strive to do, then, is to order his heart in a particular way that will give spiritual pride as little to grab hold of as possible.

Like Isaiah, a good Christian must carry in his heart a conviction that he is not a worthy servant of God. Like Abba Arsenius, a good Christian must carry in his heart a desire to be one of the flock, a member of the Church, not a lord of the Church or ruler of the Church. Unlike the monk wearing a mat in his cell, the good Christian must always realize that whatever he does is not enough and, anyway, someone else can always do more.

Even the most cursory examination of the history of the Church will show a reader that Christians have been as prone to pride as any other human beings have. This may, in fact, be the Achilles' heel of the Church, since it is the most common way in which people transgress the bounds of the Christian ideal and since it is an area in which the Church has almost completely failed to differentiate itself from the people around it.

Christian people like to **do** things to improve their Christian lives. Human beings are better at doing things than they are at ordering their hearts and minds. If we could be given specific things to **do** that would work, we might be able to fight against pride, but the only thing that will work is to "rend our hearts and not our garments"[88]. That is, we need to make an interior, spiritual change in our attitude about ourselves and our real worth, and that is very difficult for us. Adam and Eve in the Garden were very clearly tripped up by their pride when the snake tempted them with the knowledge of Good and Evil.[89] Their shortcoming was not so much the result of the fact that they did not do what they were commanded as it was that they could not order their hearts as they should have done. They were overcome from the inside, not the outside.

The Desert Tradition suggests, through its stories, that we turn our minds and hearts to reflecting on stories that describe the successes enjoyed by those who have been able to tame their hearts of pride, to some extent, at least. Stories from the Bible, lives of saints, and stories from the Desert itself all contain examples of this method of teaching. Over time, through repeated exposure to reports of what we **should** be doing, we can hope that we may be able, some times at least, to rein in our pride when it manifests itself and to turn our thoughts and actions into better channels. This is a burden that lightens only for the most advanced Christians, and it is one that all of us must try to bear, no matter how far advanced or how unimproved our spiritual state may be.

---

[88] *Joel* 2:13
[89] *Genesis* 3:1-6

The more we struggle with pride, the more we will become aware that we are not conquering it. We may be able to stamp it down, but we will never put its fire out. This is the reason that our more advanced brothers and sisters, whom we call "saints", are always convinced of their own pridefulness: they work so hard at overcoming pride that they are always aware that it still lurks within their hearts. May we work so hard at crushing our own pride that we, too, may come to see it as always present and so to keep it a bit less active, as our elders and betters have done.

> O God the Holy Spirit, who knowest how amid the cares and occupations of our daily life we so easily forget thee, fill us with a continual sense of thy presence that we may know thee more real than anything beside, through Jesus Christ our Lord. Amen.[90]

---

[90] Fisher #38, 16 (altered)

Chapter 12

ABBA MOSES

Almighty God, give us a measure of true religion and thereby set us free from vain and disappointing hopes, from lawless and exorbitant appetites, from frothy and empty joys, from anxious, self-devouring cares, from a dull and black melancholy, from an eating envy and swelling pride, that so we be possessed of that peace which passeth all understanding; through Jesus Christ our Lord. Amen.[91]

It would be very misleading and extremely untraditional to have a series of discussions of the Desert tradition without taking a look at any individual figure. Especially as an answer to the last chapter, which emphasized the use of earlier Christians as examples in the teaching of the Desert, I would like to end with a brief consideration of Abba Moses, the Ethiopian, and his seven sayings.

Abba Moses is a one of the great figures in the early Desert tradition. He is always remembered as being a black African. The Desert movement was a mixture, racially and linguistically, socially and culturally, which is something that we can often forget. (You might recall that in last chapter we read that the monks did not share some over-dry figs with Arsenius because they thought

---

[91] Fisher #114, 35-36, (a prayer of Benjamin Whichcote 1609-1683)

he would not like them. Arsenius was one of a few early monks we know of who came from the very highest social level in the empire: the Roman senatorial class. Having Arsenius in the cell next to you in the desert would have been like sharing a bunk at camp with Louis XIV: a scary prospect for an illiterate Egyptian peasant, which is what most of the monks were.) The monks had all the trouble that people in any society tend to have when they find themselves mixing across the usual lines of race, sex and class.

Abba Moses was an Ethiopian, that is, a Negro from the southern part of the Nile Valley: what is called the Upper Nile, or what modern historians would call "Nubia". Abba Moses was not alone as a Negro Christian in the Egyptian desert, but the fact that he is always remembered as being a black African shows that the Desert movement was not color-blind and that there were not enough of his fellow Nubians among the monks to make his ethnic background unremarkable. He is a good person to consider as a follow-up to our discussion of spiritual pride since his ruling characteristic in the memory of the Desert tradition is his spiritual humility. Abba Moses was revered as one who was truly "poor in spirit".

Let us look at his "seven sayings" and then we will see how his own actions, as they are reported in the Desert writings, fit together with those ideals.[92]

> These be seven sayings which the abbot
> Moses spoke to the abbot Poemen, which, if
> any keep, whether he be set in a monastery

---

[92] cix, 160-161

or in solitude, or in the world itself, he can be saved.

1. First, as it is written, a man should love God with all his soul and all his understanding:

2. A man should love his neighbor as himself.

3. A man should mortify himself from all evil.

4. A man ought not to judge his brother in any conjuncture.

5. A man ought to do no hurt to any.

6. A man ought, before he go out from the body, to cleanse himself from all foulness of the flesh and spirit.

7. A man ought always to have a contrite and humble heart. And this can he accomplish, who looks ever on his own sins and not on his neighbour's, by the succouring grace of our Lord Jesus Christ, who with God the Father and the Holy Ghost liveth and reigneth world without end. Amen.

These rules express clearly the teaching of the Desert on Christian Life, which is nothing more than the teaching of the Christian Tradition itself. The introduction to them makes this clear by claiming that following these guidelines can save a person, no matter where he lives and no matter what form of life he lives by. (This is, by the way, a very clear indication that the monks thought that their teaching could be applied to all Christian living, not just to those who had chosen to live unmarried, ascetic lives.) We see in these rules a deep concern for the welfare and worth of one's fellow believers coupled with a command to look inside oneself to root out the sins and evil tendencies lurking there. These teachings sum up an intelligent picture of the Christian ideal of human life and conduct.

Instead of talking about them in the abstract, I would like to recite to you some stories about Abba Moses found in another collection of Desert literature and try to show you how these different stories illustrate Abba Moses' own attempt to live according to his seven rules. To do this, I have used only 5 pages in one other collection. There are many more stories about Abba Moses I have not examined, but these are representative. (In other words, I did not need to search far and wide to find stories about Abba Moses that fit his sayings. I am trying to show you that these rules are woven all through Abba Moses' life so I did not need to work hard to make the two fit together.)

Let us begin with the seventh rule first: "A man ought always to have a contrite and humble heart":[93]

> Another day when a council was being held in Scetis, the Fathers treated Moses with contempt in order to test him, saying, "Why is this black man come among us?" When he heard this he kept silence. When the council was dismissed, they said to him, "Abba, did that not grieve you at all?" He said to them, "I was grieved, but I kept silence."

---

[93] 3, 139 in Ward Alphabetical

Though he was wronged for no reason, Abba Moses did not retort or retaliate, but accepted unjust rebuke humbly. This is, of course, exactly the way that St. Paul describes himself as being treated in his *First Epistle to the Corinthians*:[94]

> We are fools for Christ's sake, but ye are wise in Christ; we are weak, but ye are strong; ye are honorable, but we are despised.
>
> Even unto this present hour we both hunger, and thirst, and are naked, and are buffeted, and have no certain dwellingplace;
>
> And labor, working with our own hands: being reviled, we bless; being persecuted, we suffer it:
>
> Being defamed, we intreat: we are made as the filth of the world, and are the offscouring of all things unto this day.

This is one of the most challenging teachings of the New Testament for people in any age, but how difficult it must have been for that one, poor man so far from his home and his own people! The Desert remembered Abba Moses as being "poor in spirit" because he demonstrated his ability to live the rules that others could only shake their heads at and wish they had strength to follow.

Now let us look at a story that speaks of cleansing oneself from "foulness of the flesh and spirit", which is rule 6:[95]

---

[94] 4:10-13, See also *Matthew* 5:11-12 for a Beatitude that addresses those who can live up to this most difficult ideal.

[95] op. cit. 5, 142

The old man[96] was asked, "What is the good of the fasts and watching such a man imposes on himself?" and he replied, "They make the soul humble. For it is written, "Consider mine affliction and my trouble, and forgive all my sins." (Ps. 25.18) So if the soul gives itself all this hardship, God will have mercy on it."

Abba Moses, together with the broader Desert tradition, speaks of a connection between spiritual afflictions and physical ones. This is the logic behind all Christian fasting: we are complex beings, made up of body and soul, so what we do, physically, affects our spiritual state, too. Abba Moses supports fasting for its spiritual side-effects, not for itself. This explains why his rule puts "foulness of flesh and spirit" into the same category. Since we are unitary individuals, the things that affect any part of us affect all of us. If we are to cleanse ourselves of foulness, we need to do it, body and soul, for it to have the desired effect. The fact that the Psalm speaks of "afflictions" together with "sins" encourages Abba Moses to connect his spiritual state to the general state of his life on earth. Religious living involves the correct ordering of all aspects of our existence.

Let us now look at the teaching that we should not judge our brother, rule 5:[97]

A brother at Scetis committed a fault. A council was called to which Abba Moses was invited, but he refused to go to it. Then the

---

[96] That is, Abba Moses. (author's note)
[97] op. cit. 2, 138-139

priest sent someone to say to him, "Come, for everyone is waiting for you." So he got up and went. He took a leaking jug, filled it with water and carried it with him. The others came out to meet him and said to him, "What is this, Father?" The old man said to them, "My sins run out behind me, and I do not see them, and today I am coming to judge the errors of another." When they heard that they said no more to the brother but forgave him.

Again we see how much their serious attempts to live good lives had taught the Desert Fathers. Abba Moses knew that we instantly forget all the bad things that we do, we "put them behind us" and do not think that they "really define what kind of people we are". Other people's faults, on the other hand, leap right out at us and offend us. We want to do something about them. We do not want to have to live with that sort of thing going on around us. We want that kind of person to shape up or clear off! This tale has much in common, of course, with the story of Jesus and the woman taken in adultery[98] except that Abba Moses carefully places himself among the ranks of the sinful when he makes his point, while Jesus merely points to the sinfulness of those in the crowd around the woman.

This whole incident is a striking example of the Desert monks **living** out the Gospel in a literal, self-conscious way and living **inside** the gospels as much as they can. This ability to show the monks that they have stumbled into a gospel story (and are not coming off very well)

---

[98] *John* 8:1-11

shows Abba Moses' wit and skill in teaching as well as his
humility. This story is well known in the Desert tradition
because it so fully embodies what the monks were really
trying to cultivate: a serious desire to live a Christian life
and a sense of one's own unworthiness.

That one story, in the mind of the Desert tradition,
would be a suitable example of both the fifth teaching
and the fourth teaching. It works for the fifth teaching
because it would be wronging the other monk for Abba
Moses to judge him when he has faults himself, and it
works for the fourth teaching because it clearly reminds
us not to judge others. In both of these applications, the
key to understanding the story is that it draws from the
monk's, that is the Christian's, awareness of his own sin
as the benchmark and beginning place for all Christian
action. Until Abba Moses has cleaned up his own sins, he
does not feel able to comment on the sins of others, and,
says the Desert and the Bible, the day will never come
when he **should** feel able to do so.

How does the Desert tradition, as seen in Abba Moses' rules, describe the goal it sets before the monk as the
purpose of the religious life? When rule 3 of Abba Moses talks about "mortify[ing] oneself from all evil", the
modern world would think of this as cutting oneself off
from the distractions of day-to-day life. We would tell
ourselves that as long as we allow ourselves to struggle
with the cares of day-to-day life, and, at the same time,
try to keep ourselves insulated from being bothered by
them, we will continue to find ourselves unable to focus
on the central concern we have set before us. We must
give up our lives to save our lives, as our Lord said,[99] and
Abba Moses is recorded as teaching the same thing:[100]

---

[99] *Matthew* 16:25, *Mark* 8:35, *Luke* 9:24 + 17:33
[100] op. cit. 11, 140-141

A brother questioned Abba Moses saying, "I see something in front of me and I am not able to grasp it." The old man said to him, "If you do not become dead like those who are in the tomb, you will not be able to grasp it."

What the brother sees is the goal of the Christian life that he desires to attain. He cannot reach it because he is bogged down in the affairs of this world. There is no greater separation on earth than between those who are dead and those who are alive, so the teaching of Abba Moses is a teaching of radical separation from the cares and concerns of the world. This is completely traditional Christian teaching, but expressed in the peculiar and unique style of the Desert monks. (Some Desert stories speak of the monks' cells as 'tombs' as a way of emphasizing this idea of dying to the world. They call their houses 'tombs' to remind themselves to live as if they were dead to the world.)

What does Abba Moses say about the need to love our neighbor, rule 2?[101]

Once the order was given at Scetis, "Fast this week." Now it happened that some brothers came from Egypt[102] to visit Abba Moses and he cooked something for them.

---

[101] op. cit. 5, 139

[102] Notice that "Egypt" means the Nile River valley. Once you leave that valley and enter the desert, you have left Egypt behind and have entered the real wilderness. (author's note)

> Seeing some smoke, the neighbors said to the
> ministers, "Look, Moses has broken the com-
> mandment and has cooked something in his
> cell." The ministers said, "When he comes,
> we will speak to him ourselves." When the
> Saturday came, since they knew Abba Moses'
> remarkable way of life, the ministers said to
> him in front of everyone, "O Abba Moses,
> you did not keep the commandment of men,
> but it was so that you might keep the com-
> mandment of God."

The ministers, who seem to be more knowledgeable
and more advanced in the spiritual life than the brothers
who accuse Abba Moses, do not blink an eye at the news
that he has broken his fast. The fast, itself, is not important and their knowledge of Abba Moses makes them sure
that he would have held to the rule unless another, higher
call arose. The primacy of neighbor over self is taken for
granted in this story to the extent that the principle is
never explained, which is clear proof of how important
putting others first, even before one's religious duties, was
in the eyes of the writers of Desert literature. Abba Moses'
example is used, even inside the story that reports it, as an
example of the proper way to approach living a Christian
life. This is another good example of how the Desert likes
to teach by telling stories. This story has characters who
are already using the story, itself, to teach!

It is fitting that, as we approach the end of our time
in the Desert, we notice again the emphasis of the Tradition on the fact that care for others comes before our
individual religious practice. This is, of course, exactly
the teaching of the Parable of the Good Samaritan, and
is expressed in very much the same sort of story. The Desert Fathers loved to hand down stories that showed that
the great saints of the Desert lived lives that echoed the

life of Jesus because those stories demonstrated that this mirroring of Christ was still possible, then, and, as their handing down of the stories suggests, is still possible for us, now. The Desert Fathers may have run away from daily interaction with the world at large, but they never tried to run away from the responsibilities owed by one human being to another.

We come at the end, then, to the need to love God "with all [our] souls and with all [our] understanding". This is the idea with which every Christian meditation should begin and the teaching with which every Christian instruction should end. The summary of the Law, originally found in the Old Testament[103], which Jesus approves at the beginning of His telling of the Parable of the Good Samaritan[104] reminds us of this fact very directly.

This awareness of the need for us to keep focused on God is both a sign-post for daily practice and a reproach when we do not live up to it. This feeling of having failed in our basic duty is found in the following story, which also offers a solution to that failure's burden.

> The old man was asked, "What should a man do in all the temptations and evil thoughts that come upon him?" The old man said to him, "He should weep and implore the goodness of God to come to his aid, and he will obtain peace to the praise with discernment. For it is written, 'With the Lord on my side I do not fear. What can man do to me?'" (Ps 118.6) [105]

If we love the Lord with all our soul and understanding, we will be fixed on Him, both mentally and spiritually. Our souls will become more like Him through the

---

[103] *Deuteronomy* 6:4-5
[104] *Luke* 10:25-37
[105] op. cit. 6, 142

time we spend in His presence and our minds will be conformed to Him by keeping Him in our thoughts. As we continue on in this process, we will be more and more connected to God and less and less dependent on the world around us, so its concerns and opinion of us will recede in our sight.

It is fitting to end a talk on Abba Moses with a quote from the Psalms, just as it is fitting to end a series of chapters on the Desert Fathers with a quote from the Psalms. It reminds us of the fact that the goal of the Desert Fathers was nothing more than to live out the teaching of the Bible as fully as they possibly could. The life of the Desert, whether lived in the third and fourth centuries or lived in the modern West today, is a scriptural, evangelical life. That is, it is a life lived in and through the Gospel.[106]

The Desert Fathers may seem far away to us, but, in spirit, they are as close as we are to each other. They were a group of men and women who desperately wanted to live fully Christian lives in a world that seemed to make no place for that. Without being overly dramatic, I think it is safe to say that the world that we know and live in, now, does not seem to make much place for serious Christian life, either.

---

[106] The Christian life, if it is lived to the full, is always an evangelical life. Sometimes we allow ourselves to be convinced that there are "Evangelical" Christians and there are "Catholic" Christians and that these are different groups. Instead, the truth is that anyone who is not an evangelical Christian is, also, not a catholic Christian for 'catholic' means 'including everything' and if we do not include what is 'evangelical' in our lives then we are not catholic. If we claim to be evangelical and do not also include in our religion what is "catholic", then we are not "evangelical", either, for the gospel, the "evangel", requires of us all that it includes, and nothing less.

Just as secular Christians in the ancient world loved to hear the stories of the Desert Fathers and Mothers and to reflect on them, which is why the amount of literature their movement produced is so large and so varied, so can we, today, benefit greatly from reflecting on these witnesses of serious Christian life. Not all of us are called to the Desert, and not all those who are called to the Desert need, necessarily, to pick up and leave the lives they are living now. It is possible to live a religious life while also living a life involved in the world. There is a long tradition of doing this that goes back, in fact, to before the earliest traces of the Desert movement that we know of, as we saw when we looked at the Covenanters before we reached the Desert.

As the rules of Abba Moses claim: any of us, in any walk of life, can set ourselves to live the Desert life and follow the Gospel rules. How we do it will vary greatly and many, perhaps all, of those around us will not realize what we are trying to do. But God, Who sees in secret[107], will read the intention of our hearts and will recognize in us true brothers and sisters of Abba Moses, who was hurt but would not fight back when men said "all manner of evil against [him], falsely, for [Christ's] sake[108], of Abba Arsenius, who was rich and educated but wanted only to be at one with his Christian brothers (as Psalm 133 teaches us to desire), and even, for some of the most advanced of us, of Abba Joseph in the first story we heard who, if he wanted to, could make himself be "all fire".

These early brothers of ours were not so different from us as we might think. They wore different clothes and lived far away from us, but they loved their families (and still gave them up), enjoyed the beauties and

---

[107] *Matthew* 6:6
[108] *Matthew* 5:11-12

pleasures of the world (but tried to see beyond them) and struggled with their failed attempts at overcoming temptation (and tried not to be down-hearted). They can be examples to us of perseverance and of courage and of good cheer. Their stories can be our companions as we reflect on our lives and on theirs. Their prayers can mingle with ours as we try to worship the God they worshiped and to love the Lord they loved. If we are judged by the company we keep[109], I am sure that their company will do us as much good as anyone's could.

> Grant to us, O Lord, to know that which is worth knowing, to love that which is worth loving, to praise that which can bear with praise, to hate what in thy sight is unworthy, to prize what to thee is precious, and above all to search out and to do what is well-pleasing unto thee; through Jesus Christ our Lord. Amen.[110]

---

[109] See Psalm 15. We should remember that it told us that our company is important.

[110] Fisher #113, 35, (a prayer of Thomas á Kempis)

ST FRANCIS OF ASSISI

Chapter 13

INTRODUCTION

The first thing we need to mention, when we begin to talk about St. Francis, is the question of why we choose to talk about him when there are so many Christian examples from the past that we could consider. As a matter of fact, we might have decided not to speak about St. Francis because we thought we know too much about him already. There might be other people from whom we could learn more because we would start off without any knowledge of them. If we already have a good sense of what Francis was up to and what he taught, we might be better off taking up a study of someone who can show us something we do not already know. Well, I do not think that that is the case.

It may be that, as we go along, we will discover that we do not know St. Francis as well as we thought we did. Our rosy ideas of St. Francis as the man who loved birds and bunnies may turn out to be a sweet dream. It is only fair to say that it is not just my own jaundiced mind that thinks this way. Here is the first sentence in a book written by an Anglican bishop, who was a great scholar of St. Francis and the Franciscan movement:[111]

> St. Francis is a much-loved figure; but he was, in fact, a very terrifying person.

---

[111] Richest, 13

As we go along through these chapters, I think we will discover that Bishop Moorman was correct. Francis was not the gentle soul we think we know. He was, however, one of the most individual and striking Christian figures to appear in the history of the Western Church and there are a number of reasons why we can very profitably spend some time thinking about him.

First, Francis provides us with a personal example of Christian devotion, while also spurring us to think again about some central things because of His unique approach to pursuing Christian perfection.

Second, we have good sources for the life of St. Francis. There are a number of eyewitness accounts of his life and a great deal of very early material exists (and is available in English translation as well). There is good information open to us about St. Francis.[112]

Third, St. Francis, though he is best known in the West, of course, shows characteristics that are, in fact, more usually found elsewhere in the Christian church. It is not surprising that, among Christians outside the western stream of Christianity, Francis of Assisi is one of the most popular western saints. The qualities that make him seem so unusual to us are exactly those that make him familiar to our Eastern and Oriental brethren.

Fourth, the appeal of St. Francis beyond the bounds of Latin Christianity brings us to a very important point for us to consider. Especially in the United States, Christians live in a more mixed environment than they have in any period of the Church's history. We can find, on one

---

[112] The bibliography for these chapters contains a lot of good material. I have tried to provide brief notes that will help you choose books that are likely to contain what you are seeking.

street in our country, churches whose traditions go back to Scotland, Germany and France side-by-side with those that stem from Egypt, Ethiopia, Iraq, and even China. It is incumbent upon us to be knowledgeable about the parts of our own tradition that can help us reach out beyond our tradition's bounds to connect with Christians from other parts of the world who have very different histories.

Fifth, Francis is a good example of Christian living for us to keep in mind. This is true, in part, because he never thought that everyone should live the way he was convinced that he was called to live. In other words, Francis was an individual pursuing an unusual vocation who did not think that his own life should be imitated by everyone around him. That, in itself, is worth thinking about, in my opinion. Being certain that you are living your own vocation correctly does not mean that anyone else is called to it. "Now there are diversities of gifts, but the same Spirit"[113], said St. Paul, and Francis also knew that important truth.

How should we approach the task of getting to know Francis? We might follow his life in chronological order. That approach usually seems obvious to us. However, I think it will be easier for you to keep things straight if we approach him thematically, instead. What themes should we choose as our central focus? Fortunately, Francis himself provides a key that may be more helpful than just sticking to a chronological scheme. It is clear in all our sources that St. Francis taught his followers that there were four principal needs for the kind of Christian life

---

[113] *1 Corinthians* 12:4

that he was undertaking: humility, simplicity, a love of poverty and prayer. I think it will work best if we take those four elements as guidelines for the four central chapters in our study.

At the end of our time with him, we will try to pull all these elements together to take a look at Francis's life and what followed after it to see, as well as we can, what the impact of his life really was, for Christianity, and how we should evaluate it as we look back on it, as a whole. St. Francis was a pebble thrown into the Church by God to disturb its smooth, settled surface, but he might turn out to have been a pebble that made a few ripples and then was forgotten. What does it all add up to? Well, we will think about that later. For now, the first question to ask ourselves is: what was Francis trying to do? Bishop Moorman says,[114]

> Francis was convinced that to be a Christian was to be like Christ, and that to be a perfect Christian was to follow Christ in every possible way.

That line should echo in your minds for the whole of the time you think about St. Francis:

> "Francis was convinced…that to be a perfect Christian was to follow Christ in every possible way".

To help get you oriented and to give you a backdrop against which to view the stories you will read, let me

---

[114] Richest, 62

give you a ten minute biography of St. Francis--the kind of thing you would get if we were riding somewhere on a bus and you wanted me to tell you about the life of St. Francis.

Francis was born in 1182 in Assisi, a small city north of Rome in central Italy. He was baptized "John" but his father insisted on calling him "Francis", which means "the Frenchman", apparently because he had just come back from France and had liked it very much. Francis's family was quite well-to-do, they were merchants--middle-class people, which Italy had already developed. He was not a nobleman or a member of the upper class.

When he was 20 years old Francis was involved in a war against the nearby city of Perugia. He was captured and spent a year in prison, during which time he was the life and soul of the party, as far as we can tell. He was very sick when he was released from prison. Two years later he went off to war again, apparently in hopes of becoming a knight, but had a visionary experience on the way to the muster and turned around and returned home, which embarrassed him a great deal. He had always wanted to be a knight, so his staying out of a war caused a lot of talk.

Two years after that, at the age of 24, Francis underwent what was later commonly known as his "conversion" (though it seems to me that it would make more sense to think of his conversion as having been what happened earlier, on the way to that second war). His conversion consisted of this: he received a vision while praying in the Church of St. Damian outside of Assisi. The figure of Christ on the Cross spoke to him. Jesus said, "Francis, rebuild my church". (This is that painted cross that is so famous now. The Cross in the church was really an icon of

Christ on the Cross, painted on wood cut in the shape of a Cross.) As a result of this experience, he turned many of his father's possessions over to the poor. His father grew angrier and angrier with him because he was more and more "improvident" (or, as we would say, since it's not our money, "generous") and eventually this led to a break between them. At the final stage of this estrangement, Francis, in a famous gesture, took off all of his clothes in the public square in the presence of the bishop of Assisi and declared that he would have no father on earth, only a Father in heaven.

Two years after his call in St. Damian's Church, time which he had spent at prayer and in the hard labor of rebuilding chapels and churches near Assisi that had fallen into ruin, Francis was particularly struck by the Gospel lesson while he was attending service at the little church of the Portiuncula, which stands near to Assisi on the plain below the city. We know that the Gospel lesson was one of the passages in which Jesus sends His disciples out to preach in the world, but we do no know exactly which one. Because of this, he set out as an itinerant preacher of repentance to the people in the area around where he was living. Over the course of the next year or so he was joined by his first followers, apparently as a result of this public preaching. (It is important to keep in mind that Francis had a religious calling and had separated himself off for religious life before he began the sort of public actions that made him so much the center of attention for the rest of his life. His public life was not, in his own mind, something he thought up; it was, rather, something he was specifically commanded to do. Also, being a public figure was not a necessary part of a religious calling, even in his own experience.)

In 1209, at the age of 27, he wrote his first Rule for his Order, which he took to Rome, together with his followers (he had 11 at that point, so they were 12 in all). It seems very likely that Francis waited until he had a new 12 to mirror Jesus' original 12. He received the permission of the pope, Innocent III (pope 1198-1216), to found his order and to have his order be a recognized part of the Catholic Church. Soon after this, he began sending his followers out on preaching missions in Italy.

The Order grew by leaps and bounds, including the reception of St. Clare, a noblewoman of Assisi, three years after the recognition of the order. This marked the beginning of the Order of the Poor Ladies, who are usually called the "Poor Clares". Their order is referred to as the "Second Order of Franciscans".

In 1217, the first general chapter of all friars (the word means "brothers") was held in Assisi. Missions were planned to Germany and other countries. Provinces, that is, large administrative areas within the Order, were set up and ministers were appointed to oversee them.

In 1219, Francis, after a number of attempts, finally made his way to Egypt and paid a visit to the Sultan there, in hopes of converting him. He returned to Italy the next year and found that things in the Order were not at all to his liking. He resigned the leadership of the Order and retired, as much as he could, into private life.

In 1221 he wrote another Rule for the friars and also a Rule for the members of the Third Order, originally called "the Order of Penitence", who were people who stayed in their regular lives with their families but wanted to have a rule of life and be among the followers of Francis. This was one of the first times that provision for that approach had been made by a religious order in the West and it is an important piece in the Francis puzzle.[115]

Two years after that, in 1223, he composed a Second Rule, hoping to help organize the Order as it exploded in size. In 1224, he received the stigmata, the wounds of Christ, on his body while at prayer during Lent. And, in 1226, on the third of October, he died at the Portiuncula outside Assisi. Two years later he was canonized, and two years after that his body was put to rest in the great double Basilica, which was built for it on one end of the city of Assisi, high up on the hill. He had lived 44 years.

The parts of his life story that it is important for us to keep especially in mind, it seems to me, are:

- his early aspirations to be a knight, the fact that he was converted by hearing a Gospel reading to an outward-looking religious life from an inward-looking one,
- the fact that he gathered followers,
- the writing of the primitive Rule,
- the sending of Missions out into the world,
- his trip to the East, and
- the creation of the Third Order.

There are many of the human aspects of his life that we could dwell on, but they would tend to tell us only about Francis, himself. These few aspects just listed were chosen for their lasting importance in the Church and for the light they shed on Francis.

That is enough for us to have in mind as we begin our process of thinking about St. Francis. As we look at

[115] See History, esp. 40-45.

the specific details of his life, it is important that you keep the general trend of his life in mind. Our goal is to organize the information in a way that will help us understand it better. Let me say again that all of Francis's life was intended to be an imitation of Jesus Christ in the most literal way, and it can only be understood in that light. It is very important to be aware of this and very important that you recall it to your mind when you read something about him that seems unexpected or bizarre. This point, his desire to imitate Christ, is the keystone of Francis's life.

If you are looking for one single source to read about Francis, the most obvious and traditional place to turn would surely be St. Bonaventure's *Life of Francis*. This is one of the classic spiritual works of the western Church. It has many things to offer the reader and is an important source for our knowledge of Francis. It has the advantage of being written with access to firsthand knowledge while also representing, and in some way forming, the tradition of our knowledge about St. Francis. However, you must read it intelligently and critically. As Bishop Moorman says of this life:[116]

> No one can deny that Bonaventura's *Life of Saint Francis* is a noble and beautiful work. It gives us a charming, and in many ways faithful, portrait of the Saint as the humble imitator of Christ, the example of Gospel perfection, the founder of a great Order of men (and women) dedicated to the service of God

---

[116] ANF, 8

and man. It is only when we compare it with what we know of Saint Francis from other sources-all of them well known to Bonaventura himself-that we see how inadequate it is. As one critic has said: the aim of Bonaventura's life was "to make the Saint evermore saintly". So, in pursuit of this aim, homely little incidents were suppressed; Francis becomes less unconventional; strange, inexplicable traits in his character are passed over, and incidents which might appear undignified are omitted. The dirty, patched tunic of St. Francis is washed and ironed, and a Saint is turned out worthy to take his place in even the most fastidious company. It is a very nice Saint indeed, but it is not the man whom Leo and his friends had known and loved.

If you read Bonaventure's work, then, you should be very glad for what you have, but very careful how you receive it. We will look beyond it for much of the material about Francis we will discuss but Bonaventure is inescapably in the back of the mind of all later people who try to come closer to Francis. This need not be a difficulty if we are aware of it and can, in fact, be an advantage if we use his organization to help us see the outline of things clearly while reserving our assent to Bonaventure's judgments until our own minds are made up.

The goal of these chapters is to get as clear a sense of Francis' own beliefs and aims as we can. It would be much easier, as an historical project, to look at what the movement he began has become but our interest is in the life and teachings of its founder, rather than in how others have responded to them.

We are trying to get a sense of St. Francis, the human being. We want to know Francis Bernadone, the Christian penitent. In order to do that we must see him as he lives, and hear him as he speaks and try to view him as clearly as we can. We want to see, as clearly as possible, what he offers as an example of fervent Christian living, and in order to do that, we will have to focus on Francis, himself. He makes a fascinating subject of study.[117]

> O Lord, support us all the day long of this troublous life, until the shadows lengthen and the evening comes, and the busy world is hushed, and the fever of life is over, and our work is done. Then, Lord, in thy mercy grant us a safe lodging, and a holy rest, and peace at the last. Amen.

---

[117] BCP, 594-595 altered

Chapter 14

HUMILITY

> O God, whose nature and property is ever to have mercy and to forgive; Receive our humble petitions; and though we be tied and bound with the chain of our sins, yet let the pitifulness of thy great mercy loose us; for the honour of Jesus Christ, our Mediator and Advocate. *Amen.*[118]

Humility is the first of the themes in St. Francis's life that we will examine. Francis himself understood this as the beginning and basis of the way he was called to live. This humility sprang from penitence, and penitence was woven into the hearts of Francis and his companions from the very beginning. When the very first followers of Francis went out into the surrounding towns and were asked who they were and what they were doing, they replied:[119]

We are Penitents, from the city of Assisi.

While many of us may think that people who have a lively sense of their own sins and try to do something about it are unusual and memorable people, Francis did not think that these things he and his companions did were worthy of special respect; quite the reverse, in fact:[120]

---

[118] BCP, 63
[119] Englebert, 53
[120] Bonaventure, 6.3, 58

He often used to tell the friars: "No one should flatter himself for doing anything a sinner can also do. A sinner," he said, "can fast, pray, weep and mortify his flesh. This one thing He cannot do: be faithful to his Lord. Therefore we should glory in this: if we give back to the Lord the glory that is his, if we serve him faithfully and ascribe to him whatever He gives to us."

It is very important for us to understand Francis's point here. Any Christian who focuses very hard on self-improvement can fall into the trap of thinking that he can save himself through his own exertions. Because Francis worked so hard at **doing** things, we must be sure that we realize that Francis clearly teaches that, since anyone can perform religious actions, they do not set one apart. The faith that motivates you to do them is the important thing. Francis in no way thought that his austere life could earn him salvation. That was not a possibility, in his mind, and should never be a part of our view of him.

Bonaventure, at the beginning of Chapter 12 in his *Life*[121], describes Francis worrying over whether he should spend his time and effort in preaching or in individual religious practice. He asked the friars who were closest to him what they thought he should do, explaining his reasons for being uncertain. He sent messengers to Brother Sylvester and to St. Clare to see what advice they had for

---

[121] Bonaventure, 125-129. This story is too long to include in the chapter but is an attractive example of Franciscan thought on prayer and public ministry.

him. When all the answers came back the same: that he should continue to preach publicly as he had been doing, Francis accepted it as a sign that all these people had been inspired by the Holy Ghost and, after that, he felt no more uncertainty. This story is very important for any attempt to figure out what was motivating Francis. The anecdote shows us that Francis wanted to be guided by the Holy Spirit. That is why he was waiting for, and heeding, the Holy Spirit's voice. This is not the approach of someone who thinks of himself as an independent agent, separate from God's action in the world. It is, rather, the instinct of someone who sees himself as dedicated to working together with God, and for God, in the world. This helps us to see clearly what he must have understood his ascetical practices to be: a way to help him work with God more closely than he could otherwise. All the things he did were pieces of his larger effort to accomplish this single great goal.

This attitude of Francis: that he saw himself as trying to further the grace of God in the world, reached all the way to the core of his being. All the sources show that Francis was happiest when he could focus all his time and attention on worshipping God and trying to draw closer to Him, but almost all of his life after his conversion was spent in outward-directed actions in the hope of helping others to commit themselves to trying to know God better. This was Francis's vocation, but it was not the desire of his heart.

In some ways, Francis's public life was all one expression of humility, for it forced him to put aside the life he yearned for (and enjoyed) in order to do something he felt he did poorly, but that he knew was for the benefit of others. The difficulty of finding a way to balance individual religious practice with a public presence in the Church is something that all followers of religious life have wrestled with, at all periods in the Church's history. The pure ascetic flees the public life of the Church completely and does not worry about a public role in the greater Church, at all. We know that the desire to do this was circulating among the early group of Franciscans, because it is expressed vividly by Brother Giles, one of the earliest and purest examples of the true follower of Francis:[122]

> "The true religious", he declared, "ought to be like wolves, which never show themselves in public unless necessary."

Left to his own devices, Francis would have liked to have been one of those religious wolves, but God did not leave him alone, so he spent his life working for others' religious benefit more than for his own.

Francis's desire that his Order should foster and exemplify humility found expression in many areas that might seem odd to us. For example, his concern about the place of Learning in the Order sprang from a conviction that study involved hierarchy. Hierarchy, Francis thought, would always work against the complete, shared humility that was his ideal for the Order. (We will return to this later, but keep it in the back of your mind.)

It is important for us to understand that Francis's focus on humility came from his conviction that only by living humbly would he be able to draw closer to God. As Bishop Moorman says, in his biography of St. Francis:[123]

---

[122] Englebert, 100
[123] Biography, 39

We shall misunderstand the spirit of St. Francis completely if, for one moment, we forget that his whole desire was to please God and to live in the closest touch with him. Books have been written on Francis as the inaugurator of what is called "the Social Gospel"; and it is, of course, true that he did arouse the consciences of men to the miseries of the poor and the lepers. But the mainspring of his life was not compassion for his fellow man but intense love of God from which naturally flowed not only love for man but for all creatures. All that Francis accepted, and bore, and suffered was in obedience to what he knew to be the will of God.

That obedience to the will of God, which Moorman focuses on, is nothing other than an expression of Francis's attempts to live out humility in his relationship with God. Humility drove him away from the life that he desired, and toward the life for which he became famous, exactly because his primary concern was God. His concern for others was secondary, but it consumed his life because it was a way to live humbly, a way to imitate Jesus and because he was commanded to live that way by Christ from the Cross. This focus on other people that overtook so much of his life is vividly expressed by this observation of Bishop Moorman:[124]

---

[124] Biography, 78

If Francis could choose the sort of
stained-glass window which he would like
to be erected in his memory he was certainly
choose one which depicted him surrounded
not by birds and butterflies, but by the sick
and the leprous, by cripples and tramps, by
all the dregs of society whose life he so brave-
ly shared and whose souls he so dearly loved.

This brings us to the topic of Francis's attempt to
imitate the life of Jesus. As I said in the last chapter,
this effort lies behind every detail of his life. We need
to understand and imagine Francis and his early followers hearing the Gospel stories, especially in the synoptic
gospels (*Matthew, Mark* and *Luke*), and taking them to
heart as an example to be followed in every detail. Many
things in Francis's life can only be understood properly
if we keep this in mind. To take an example that might
(misleadingly) make Francis seem very much like a modern Lutheran minister, let us think about his invention of
the Christmas pageant.

During one of his Advent periods of devotion in the
very last part of his life, when he was very sick, St. Francis
went apart from the other brothers to undertake an organized retreat. This is how Bp. Mormon describes it:[125]

At Greccio Francis tried to find solace and
peace. His mind was filled with thoughts of
Christ's earthly life as he pictured each scene,

---

[125] Biography, 100-101. cf. Englebert, 232

and as Christmas drew near he determined to stage a re-enactment of the scene at Bethlehem on the night of Christ's nativity. "There was in that place", says Celano[126] "a man named John, of good repute but better life, whom the blessed Francis loved with special affection." A fortnight before Christmas Francis sent for him and told him that he wished "to make a memorial of that child who was born in Bethlehem, and in some sort behold with bodily eyes his infant hardships, how he lay in a manger on the hay, with the ox and the ass standing by". So John made the necessary preparations-a stable with the beast standing there, a manger full of hay, and in the midst an altar where the holy mysteries might be celebrated. And there, in those simple and homely surroundings, at midnight, Mass was said with Francis serving as deacon and reading the Gospel with such devotion that men and women wept with joy.

The point of this exercise was not for Francis to see the little children of the neighborhood dressed up in their bathrobes with tinsel around their heads, "oh so cute". (I love cute children and have three of them, myself.) This was designed as an aid to devotional contemplation so that Francis could better understand the depth and fullness of the humility of God the Son in being born into this world in such humble surroundings.[127]

---

[126] Thomas of Celano wrote both of the first two official lives of St. Francis. They can be found in Habig, 177-616. Habig provides an introduction and notes, to make them easier to understand.
[127] History, 256-257

…Thomas of Celano says that 'above all things, the humility of the Incarnation and the love of the Passion so occupied his mind that he could scarcely think of anything else'. As he thought of the birth of Jesus he wept in contemplation of the poverty and squalor of the stable and of the consequent sufferings both of the Mother and of the infant Christ; and though the Feast of the Nativity of the Lord was always to him the *festum festorum*[128] which brought him great joy, there always lay, behind the joy, a deep and poignant sorrow that the Christ should suffer from the very beginning of his life, that beyond the stable lay the cross, and that all this was done because of human sin and forgetfulness of God. Hence equally dear to him, though more terrible in its emotional appeal, was the Passion. As he could enter, with shepherds and magi, into the stable of Bethlehem and kneel in wonder before the crib, so he could stand at the foot of the cross, with Mary and John, and live through all the agony of those hours. It was to this end that he prayed, on La Verna, that he might feel in his own body and soul 'the pain that thou, sweet Lord, didst bear in the hour of thy most bitter passion', and could teach others to pray that they might 'die for love of thy love as thou didst deign to die for love of my love'.

---

[128] Latin for "the feast of feasts". (author's note)

St. Francis made a great point of emphasizing the fact that the consecration of the elements in the Holy Communion recreates and reenacts the humility of God the Son at the Incarnation because it brings God the Son, in reality, into the world again, in His Body and Blood, found in the bread and wine.[129] This celebration of the Eucharist in the midst of the manger scene is a careful acting-out of this theological conviction. Francis is making a profound theological and christological point by doing this. In some ways, it is a romantic gesture, but in other ways it is a theological laboratory experiment and can only be understood if we realize that its focus is the humility of God and Francis's attempt to express his devotion for that, rather than anything else that might move us to have a Christmas pageant in our local church each Winter.

Here is another example of Francis's insistence on humility as a cardinal quality of the members of his Order. This is a long story, but it shows the value Francis placed on humility so clearly that I think it is worth the space to include it.[130]

---

[129] A quotation from a letter of St. Francis to the friars that emphasizes this element in his spiritual understanding can be found at Richest, 60-61:
"Our whole being should be seized with fear, the whole world should tremble and heaven rejoice, when Christ the Son of the living God is present on the altar in the hands of the priest. What wonderful majesty! What stupendous condescension! O sublime humility! O humble sublimity! That the Lord of the whole universe, God and the Son of God, should humble himself like this and hide under the form of a little bread for our salvation."
[130] ANF, 31-33

Brother Conrad records that in the friary at Milan was a brother who had been received into the Order by Saint Francis in this
way. Two brothers were living with a learned
man who, seeing them, began to ask them
about their way of living. So they showed
him the Rule, since it was the custom of the
older friars to carry the Rule about with them
wherever they went. When the learned man
saw that the Rule bore the very essence of the
Gospels, he, as a man taught and inspired by
God and learned in all knowledge, realized
that it was the work of the Holy Spirit, ordained and composed by St. Francis at the
dictation of Christ. So he said: "Brothers, I
wish to join your Order". And they answered:
"My lord, we have a father, Brother Francis,
who receives all who wish to follow our way
of life. You must go to him at Assisi to the
place called S. Mary of the Angels, and we
will ask him to receive you."

So he did all that the brothers told him,
and in due course came to Assisi, where he
found St. Francis and the brother who had
promised to help him. Now, he came with
much luggage and well dressed and mount-
ed. When the brothers recognized him they
told the Blessed Francis that a very learned
man was coming to join the brotherhood.
So Francis told them to bring him into the
place where he was with the brothers, and
in his presence he said: "Brothers, this man
wishes to become one of us. What do you

think about it?" And he began with the friar who had advised the man to come and who had spoken to Saint Francis about him. And the blessed Francis said: "Brother, what do you think about it? Shall I receive him?" And he answered: "No, Father, I should say not". And Francis asked all the other brothers the same question, and they all made the same reply.

Then Francis said to the brothers: "Brethren, you have well said, for neither does it seem to me that he ought to become one of us. But if you had all told me to receive him I would have had him." Then the friar who had been the first to answer said to the blessed Francis: "Father, do you know what I think? I think that if this man is prepared to be cook to the friars we should have him, otherwise not." Then the blessed Francis asked all the brothers what they thought of this suggestion. And they all agreed with it. Then Francis turned to the learned clerk and said: "Well, brother, you've heard what they say. What will you do?" But the man was speechless and astonished at what the brother had said. First he said that he did not know what to say. But finally he said: "Yes, I am willing to be your cook and anything else that you tell me".

Then the Blessed Francis took him into the Order and sent him to Rome to serve in the friars' kitchen, and there he stayed for a month. After that, the Blessed Francis or-

dered him on obedience to exercise the office
of Guardian and to preach.

Thus the Blessed Francis wished the
brethren to pass through the gate of humility,
and thus, both wise and foolish, to go from
strength to strength in pursuit of humility
until the Lord should inspire those who held
office in the Order to exalt them. Thus, by
the grace of God and the virtue of humility
(even as previously they had known something of the grace and power of God), they
might lead others as much by the quality of
their lives as by the force of their teaching
and the power of the Spirit, and so gather a
harvest of souls.

There are two very important things for us to notice in
this story. First, Francis makes use of the man's special gift
and training as soon as the learned man has proven both
to Francis's satisfaction, and to himself, that his humility
is sufficient for him to take his place as an equal member
of the Order. Francis is not wasteful of the opportunity
that the Holy Spirit has provided by bringing this man to
him. Second, the story ends with a clear indication of the
fact that the humility of the friars was understood to be
their most important preaching tool. It was by their lives
and the examples they set that Francis expected them to
have an effect on those around them and on the wider
Church. Members of the Order who were not willing to
live the lives the Order demanded could not remain in it
because they would make it impossible for any members
of the Order to succeed as Christian examples to the outside world. The followers of Francis were perceived as a

group and they would either succeed or fail as a group, together. They must all live in humility or none of them could live in humility.

Francis did not only think that humility required that one be willing to take a place below other people. His idea of humility extended, as well, to the relations of the individual Christian to the Church, as we will see a number of times in the course of his life. However, even beyond that, it reached also to the relations of Christians to God, Himself. For many Christians, perhaps for most Christians, the most difficult surrender we attempt, the most demanding form of humility, lies in our heart. It is to surrender our free will to God's direction. This seems to have been something that Francis sought very assiduously to do.

There are a number of times in Francis's life when he exhibits a desire to surrender his will to God, completely. These are some of the moments when he appears the strangest to us and the most distant. One of the most striking of these times is found in his decision to go with his first follower, Bernard, and seek the advice of God before allowing Bernard to join him in his life of self denial.[131] They go to Church, say a few prayers, and then open the Gospel book found on the altar three times, asking for God's testimony. All three of the results seem to instruct Bernard to give up his old life and to take up a new one with Francis. That is enough for both of them and off they go to spend the rest of their lives together. This practice[132] is actually one that has a very long history

---

[131] Bonaventure, 3.3, 24-25
[132] van der Horst, 143-173 in Rutgers, discusses this use of the Bible among both Jews and Christians.

in the Church. I do not know enough about St. Francis, and I am not certain that anyone knows enough about St. Francis, to know whether or not he engaged in this practice with an awareness that it was something Christians had been doing for a very long time or whether he thought it up on his own, guided, I presume, by the Holy Spirit. I do know that St. Bonaventure records that he engaged in this at least three times during his life.

Along the same lines, there is a very interesting incident that happens just at the time that Francis is leaving Italy to go to the East in search of the Sultan.[133] Francis has arrived at the port of Ancona with too many of the friars who want to go along with him to the East. Since Francis believes himself to be God's representative and to be engaged in God's work, he tries to devise a way to let God choose who should be allowed to accompany him. He asks a young boy, who is standing there, to choose who should go from the group. He asks him, "Should all these brothers go abroad with me?" The boy says not. "Which ones does God want to go with me", says Francis. The boy touches the ones he chooses, saying "This one, and this one, and this one, and this one, too, is chosen", until he has chosen eleven. (So, Francis, again, would be the twelfth. You see how the number of the Disciples reappears.) Then he says to Francis, "That's God's will." Francis says, "OK", and that is what they do.

Again, this is very much like a practice that we know took place during the early period of Christian life. We know that there were places which, when they needed to choose a new bishop and were not certain whom they

---

[133] ANF, 27-28

should choose, would write the names of all the possible candidates (churches usually being quite small then) and put them on the altar. They said a few prayers, sang a few psalms, and then asked a small child (below the age of seven and, so, in a state of Grace, as well as unable to read), to choose one of the names off the altar.[134] You can see that this was an attempt by the local Church to remove itself entirely from the selection process and make a way for God to choose on its behalf. I do not know if St. Francis was following earlier practice or just letting the Spirit lead him as he went along through life. I do know that he intended this kind of action to make God the ruler of his life and to be an expression of the humility he was trying to live out before the face of God.

That gives us some examples of what St. Francis meant by humility and of the ways in which he tried to act in accordance with humility during his lifetime. There are two points in particular that we should think about as we ponder this topic.

1) First, this public acting out of an imitation of Christ was clearly effective, at least to the extent of people recognizing what was being done by Francis and his followers. It is a very important point to be aware of that, for example, in England, when they first arrived, the friars were commonly known as "the Brethren of the Order of the Apostles".[135] Medieval people knew more

---

[134] Bingham, vol. 1, 424-426, discusses the choosing of bishops in the Church by lots, tracing the practice back to Acts 1, where the method is used to choose Matthias to replace Judas. He mentions that the Council of Barcelona (599 AD) describes a standard process for the application of this method, which makes it sound like an acknowledged tool of the Church.

[135] Englebert, 169

about the Bible than we give them credit for, and it was clear that the general outline of the Gospel life, as seen in the readings at worship, was recognized in the actions of the early Franciscan friars. When Francis decided that he was called to live a public life for the benefit of those around him in the Church, he clearly chose a way of doing this that was comprehensible to the surrounding Christians. In many ways, Francis was a consummate teacher, though he was never much of an author or a trained religious thinker. He taught through his actions more than through his words, but he taught in a way that people could understand.

2) The second point to keep in mind is found beautifully illustrated in this story in one of the earliest lives of St. Francis:[136]

Not only did the man of God show himself humble before his superiors; but also among his equals, and those beneath him, he was more ready to be admonished and corrected than to give admonitions. Wherefore when one day he was riding on an ass, because, weak and infirm as he was, he could not go by foot, he passed through the field of a peasant who happened to be working there just then. The peasant ran over to him and asked solicitously if he were Brother Francis. When the man of God humbly replied that

---

[136] Richest, 74-75. This is drawn from Thomas of Celano's second life of Francis.

he was the man he was talking about, the peasant said: "Try to be as good as you are said to be by all men, for many put their trust in you. Therefore I admonish you never to be other than you are expected to be". When the man of God heard this, he got down from the ass and threw himself before the peasant and humbly kissed his feet, thanking him for being kind enough to give him this warning.

It is clear that those first Franciscans were being watched, especially with an eye to seeing if they were really what they appeared to be. False humility would be worse than open pride, as far as Francis's desire to teach was concerned, and he was not the only one who knew it.

This last story shows clearly that the actions of the Franciscans were being understood by those who witnessed them in the same way that they were being performed. These early Franciscans were not self-indulgent men, working out their religious vocations with one eye in the mirror and one eye on the audience, they were people who were trying to live a certain life and also provide an example for their Christian brethren at the same time. This public religious life was something that was quite new in the Church in the Medieval West.[137] The

---

[137] There had been public saints before this time, however. The best place to start to learn about them is with Peter Brown, *Society and the Holy in Late Antiquity* Berkeley, CA: University of California Press 1982. Following Brown's lead, a great deal of work has been done in this area of early Christianity and it has greatly increased our ability to appreciate how a man like Francis could influence his society and the Church within it.

idea of a religious community living out in the world, rather than enclosed away from it, may have been the most radical thing that Francis offered to the Western Church. Only if this task were undertaken in a very particular way could it be done with humility and with the goal of fostering humility. That delicate balance, which has proven so difficult to maintain throughout the history of the Franciscan Order, was something that Francis struggled with for the whole of his religious life.[138]

> O God, by whom the meek are guided in judgment, and light riseth up in darkness for the godly; Grant us, in all our doubts and uncertainties, the grace to ask what thou wouldest have us to do, that the Spirit of Wisdom may save us from all false choices, and that in thy light we may see light, and in thy straight path may not stumble; through Jesus Christ our Lord. *Amen.*

---

[138] BCP, 595

Chapter 15

SIMPLICITY

O Almighty God, who alone canst order
the unruly wills and affections of sinful men;
Grant unto thy people, that they may love
the thing which thou commandest, and desire that which thou dost promise; that so,
among the sundry and manifold changes
of the world, our hearts may surely there
be fixed, where true joys are to be found;
through Jesus Christ our Lord. *Amen.*[139]

We now come to the second of the four cardinal
points of Francis's vision for the Christian life: simplicity. As we first look at it, "simplicity" seems to mean di-
rectness and following God's will as plainly as possible.
We will find that Francis did think that simplicity was
a direct following of God's will, but we will also see that
it had a more important place in his understanding of
how he should live than that first glance would suggest.
In order to get a sense of the depth of meaning and the
importance he credited "simplicity" with having, there
is no better way than to look at how it worked in the
lives of the very earliest Franciscans. Once we have some
examples to look at, we can try to take a step back and
make sense of them.

---

[139] BCP, 174

There was once a certain Friar who would not submit to the discipline of Obedience. So Francis called him one day and spoke very severely to him. Then he ordered the friars to strip him and to take him outside, where there was a big pit. In this the Saint made the man stand while the friars cast in earth as if to bury him alive. When the man was buried up to the chin, Francis said to him: "Are you dead yet, brother?" To which the other humbly replied: "Yes, father, or at least I deserve to die for my sins". Then the Blessed Francis ordered the friars to dig him out again, and said to him: "Get up now, brother, and if you are really dead as a good religious ought to be dead to the world and the flesh, then you will obey your superiors in everything and will never be reluctant to do what you are told, just as a corpse can't refuse to do anything". [140]

... one day in the year 1222 the Religious of Salzburg, on receiving a letter from brother Caesar directing them to be present at the provincial Chapter, "if they wished", they [sic] were plunged by these last words into deep consternation. Did their superior doubt their obedience and had he lost confidence in them? So, by common consent, they set out and walked 250 miles on foot to Speyer to clear up this mystery and protest

[140] ANF, 24-25. cf. Bonaventure 6.4

their submission. The Minister Provincial, delighted to see them again, smilingly promised to write more clearly in the future.[141]

At that time when blessed Francis was living with the brethren whom he then had, he lived in such poverty with them, that they observed the Holy Gospel in and through all things to the letter, from that day in which the Lord revealed to him that he and his brethren should live according to the form of the Holy Gospel. Whence he forbade the brother who used to cook for the friars to put dried beans in warm water when they were to be given to the friars to eat on the following day, as the custom is, so that they might observe that saying of the Holy Gospel, *take no thought for the morrow.* And so that brother put off setting them to soften until after Mattins, because by then the day in which they were to be eaten had begun.[142]

Francis's widely reported and very strictly enforced rules for his followers about avoiding money are an expression of the same concern that we see in these three stories. If it is understood properly, his avoidance of money can be seen to be a characteristic example of Francis's effort to pursue a life of simplicity. Francis was set on focusing all of his attention on imitating the Gospel life of Jesus, as far as he possibly could. One of the sayings of

---

[141] Englebert, 166
[142] Biography, 31

Christ that struck a chord most strongly in his conscience was the one cited in the third story we just saw: "take no thought for the morrow"[143]. Listen to these few verses from the Sermon on the Mount[144] and try to hear them with the ears of St. Francis. If you can hear with his ears, you will be able to see into his heart.

> No man can serve two masters: for either he will hate the one, and love the other; or else he will hold to the one, and despise the other.
>
> Ye cannot serve God and mammon.
>
> Therefore I say unto you, Take no thought for your life, what ye shall eat, or what ye shall drink; nor yet for your body, what ye shall put on. Is not the life more than meat, and the body than raiment?
>
> Behold the fowls of the air: for they sow not, neither do they reap, nor gather into barns; yet your heavenly Father feedeth them. Are ye not much better than they?
>
> Which of you by taking thought can add one cubit unto his stature?
>
> And why take ye thought for raiment? Consider the lilies of the field, how they grow; they toil not, neither do they spin:
>
> And yet I say unto you, That even Solomon in all his glory was not arrayed like one of these.

---

[143] *Matthew* 6:34
[144] *Matthew* 6:24-34

> Wherefore, if God so clothe the grass of the field, which to day is, and to morrow is cast into the oven, shall he not much more clothe you, O ye of little faith?
>
> Therefore take no thought, saying, What shall we eat? or, What shall we drink? or, Wherewithal shall we be clothed?
>
> (For after all these things do the Gentiles seek:) for your heavenly Father knoweth that ye have need of all these things.
>
> But seek ye first the kingdom of God, and his righteousness; and all these things shall be added unto you.
>
> Take therefore no thought for the morrow: for the morrow shall take thought for the things of itself. Sufficient unto the day is the evil thereof.

For Francis, there was a clear choice to be made between two masters: the World or God. Francis desired, with all his heart, to serve God, and that meant doing God's will. Jesus had said "Take no thought for the morrow", and Francis intended, with all the simplicity and intensity in his heart, to do just that. This is where his abhorrence of money came from.

Because money is not good for anything, in itself, but is only useful when it is kept and exchanged for something else, Francis understood it to be, essentially, planning ahead in concrete form. Because of that, money literally embodied exactly the approach to life that Francis was trying to avoid, and Francis's followers were instructed never to touch it and, if possible, never even to look at it, so great was its power to lead them astray into a planned, organized existence thought to be.

This might seem like a very grim way to live your life, but many of the stories concerning St. Francis that deal with his dedication to simplicity in following God's will are very funny. His early followers echoed this trait of his. There is a whole collection of stories about Brother Juniper, often attached to the end of the *Little Flowers* [145], that really is nothing other than religious comedy. Francis was, among other things, very consciously acting as what we would call "a performance artist". That is to say, that, like Jesus before him, he realized that acting out his convictions and teachings could often be a better way of communicating them than merely expressing them in words. He did not invent this teaching technique, of course. Jesus did it before him, and Jeremiah did it before Jesus[146]. This teaching through action is something that many earlier saints knew how to do, too. We have many

---

[145] *The Little Flowers* of St. Francis is a collection of stories about him and his companions that has been one of the best loved and most read spiritual books in western Christianity. Because it is completely unsystematic and assumes that the reader knows a great deal about St. Francis, it is not a very good place for a modern reader to begin getting to know Francis. *The Little Flowers* was written during the Middle Ages, too, so one needs some knowledge of that time to be able really to appreciate the stories. Still, for the reader who is ready for it, *The Little Flowers* is a source of great delight.

[146] The scene in Chapter 28 of *Jeremiah* in which the prophet Hananiah breaks the yoke for the shoulders of Jeremiah as a symbol of God's promise to take Nebuchadnezzar from the necks of the nations is a good example of his use of this approach to teaching. Jeremiah is not unique among the prophets in this regard. *Isaiah* 20 tells of Isaiah receiving a direct command from the Lord to go naked and barefoot for three years as a sign of what was to come for Egypt at the hands of Assyria. Francis was on well-trodden ground when he used actions to teach.

saints' lives from the early Church that show them behaving in just this way.

It is one thing, of course, to know that earlier Christians have acted a certain way, but it is something quite different to encounter that sort of behavior in your own life. Many of Francis's actions were surprising and shocking to the people who witnessed them, and Francis seems to have intended to cause that reaction.

There is a very striking story along these lines that deals with the first meeting between Francis and the Pope when Francis had journeyed to Rome to try to receive the Church's blessing for his new order. (We should notice, by the way, that both Francis and the Pope are consciously acting out their roles in public. Francis was not the only one who knew how to make a point through his behavior.)[147]

> The reception was, at first, very chilly, if we are to believe Matthew of Paris. This contemporary chronicler relates that going into the Lateran Palace, Francis walked in unceremoniously and went up to where the Pope was. But he looked so shabby with "his poor tunic, his tangled locks, and his great black eyebrows," that Innocent III pretended to take him for a swineherd.
>
> "Leave me alone with your Rule!" said he. "Go find your pigs instead. You can preach all the sermons you want to them!"

---

[147] Englebert, 63

Francis did not wait to be told twice. He dashed to a pigsty, smeared himself with dung, and reappeared before the Pope.

"My lord," he said, "now that I have done what you commanded, please be good enough to grant me my request".

The Pontiff had to admit that this petitioner did not appear to be a rebel. So, "thinking it over", writes Matthew, "he regretted having given him so ill a reception: and after sending him away to wash up, promised him another audience."

It is a mistake to confuse this simplicity of Francis with stupidity. Francis certainly knew that the Pope was deeply concerned about the rise of uncontrolled charismatic groups in the Church. He was, after all, going to Rome in order to receive its blessing because of this very fact. (Francis could be practical, too, if he wanted. He knew that, if his group were publicly seen to be accepted by the official Church, they could fulfill their function and follow their vocation much more easily and satisfactorily.) When the Pope flippantly made an unreasonable request of Francis, his running to fulfill it at that very moment was a concrete way of showing the Pope that he had no desire to separate himself from the Church's authority. This story, whether true or not, demonstrates both Francis's simplicity and his intelligence in arranging to follow his vocation within the Church in which he lived.

This next example, which describes St. Francis's unwillingness to have the members of the order founded by Saint Clare called "sisters", the common term for nuns, may seem to be a trivial thing. But, as we have

seen, Francis clung with great tenacity to the clear word
of the Gospel text. Since what he was trying to do: live
a true Gospel life, was a very difficult and uncertain en-
terprise, Francis held tenaciously to what was obvious in
the Gospel whenever he could see it. This story is best
understood as a good example of that desire to hold to
the clear commands at all costs. In order to understand
this story you must have in mind the instruction of Jesus
found, for example, in *The Gospel according to St. Matthew* 10:34-38:

> Think not that I am come to send peace
> on earth: I came not to send peace, but a
> sword.
> For I am come to set a man at variance
> against his father, and the daughter against
> her mother, and the daughter in law against
> her mother in law.
> And a man's foes shall be they of his own
> household.
> He that loveth father or mother more
> than me is not worthy of me: and he that
> loveth son or daughter more than me is not
> worthy of me.
> And he that taketh not his cross, and fol-
> loweth after me, is not worthy of me.

With that in mind, we turn to St. Francis.

> Brother Stephen used to say that the
> Blessed Francis would never be intimate with
> any woman nor would he accept familiarity
> from any of them. Saint Clare was the only

one for whom he showed any affection. But when he spoke to her or about her he would never use her name, but called her simply "Christiana". He had always charge of her and of her convent. Nor would he ever allow any other convent to be made, although during his lifetime other houses were in fact founded by the influence of others. And when Saint Francis heard that the women who lived in these convents were called "sisters" he was greatly disturbed and is believed to have exclaimed: "God has taken away our wives and now the devil gives us sisters".

Now the Lord Ugolino, Bishop of Ostia, who was Protector of the Order, loved these sisters very dearly. One day he said to Saint Francis as he was leaving his presence: "My brother, let me commend these ladies to you". Then Saint Francis, with a merry look, replied: "That's right, father, in future they shall not be called 'lesser sisters', but 'ladies', as you now term them in commending them to me". And from that day they were known as "ladies" not "sisters".[148]

The "merry look" that Francis gave the bishop shows that he understood how his insistence seemed to those around him. He knew that almost everyone would think that he was making a foolish distinction to no purpose, but his desire to fulfill the plain sense of the instructions

---

[148] ANF, 35-36

of Christ was so strong that he was determined to follow his conscience. Since the Gospel did not allow people to hold family members dearer than Jesus, the cautious Christian would choose to have no family at all and so avoid the possibility of going wrong. Giving up one's immediate family only to be saddled with hundreds of 'sisters' would be to take two steps backward after having taken only one forward. So Francis avoided the problem by having his female followers be his 'ladies' instead of his 'sisters'. This would allow him to acknowledge their existence while he still held to the letter of Jesus' command in the gospels. Francis clearly had a lively sense that, on one level, the distinction he was making was absurd. That did not make him think that it was meaningless and did not turn him away from pursuing it.

This next example of simplicity, which comes in the context of a lesson in obedience for new brothers, shows his sense of the absurd very clearly.[149]

> Two young men came to the Blessed Francis desiring to be received into the Order. But the Saint, anxious to test their obedience and to find out whether they were really willing to surrender their own wills, took them into the garden and said to them: "Come, and let us plant some cabbages; and as you see me doing, so you must do also". So the Blessed Francis began to plant, putting the cabbages with the roots up in the air and the leaves down under the ground. Then one of the two men did as Francis was doing, but the other

---

[149] ANF, 33-34

said: "That isn't the way to plant cabbages, father; you're putting them in upside down!" But Francis turned and said to him: "My son, I want you to do as I do". And when the other still refused, thinking it all wrong, the Blessed Francis said to him: "Brother, I see that you are a very learned man; but go your way; you won't do for my Order". So he accepted the one and refused the other.

People who could not follow clear commands would never succeed at Francis's style of life. If he were to try to be a follower of Francis, and then were to argue with the approach of the group at every turn or even ignore it and go his own way, as he did with the cabbages, his presence would be a source of discord in the group and could serve to unsettle many of the brothers. Simplicity in obedience and simplicity in humility were the only traits that would carry one along in Francis's march toward Jesus, so the argumentative planter of cabbages was sent away. He would make a good, careful farmer but would never be single-hearted enough to be one of Francis's fools for Christ.

Of course, not all the results of following this "simple" approach to living a Gospel life were absurd. We would miss the point and devalue it unduly if we thought that simplicity was merely a spur to extravagant folly and practical joking among the Franciscans. This same simplicity could lead to behavior on the part of the friars that sprang clearly and directly from Jesus' teaching. The following story is a famous example, and it is important to know that there are many stories about Francis and his first companions that parallel this one. This behavior seems to have been the pattern that the early Franciscans followed.[150]

[150] ANF, 17-18

Once when they had arrived together at the house of a certain noble lady she devoutly offered the Blessed Francis a piece of coloured cloth suitable for making a priest's chasuble. The holy man accepted it, and shortly afterwards went to stay at a certain monastery.[151] While the Blessed Francis was having an intimate talk with the abbot, a certain lay-brother, who had been in pain for many years, lay in bed uttering the most terrible shrieks and yells and cursing everyone in the monastery for not coming to look after him. Hearing this, the Blessed Francis, with his companion, hastened to the sick man's bedside and implored him to be patient, praising the divine providence which can bring good out of people, soothing the sick man with his words, bidding him see his faults, and showing him the most loving sympathy. And seeing him lying there, naked and wretched, he said to Brother Stephen: "Bring me that cloth which the lady gave us. We shall find plenty of chasubles if need be; but this naked creature must be clothed, or how can we fulfil the law of Christ?" The good brother brought the cloth; and Francis, with his own hands, cut out a garment and sewed it together, and, before he left the place, he visited the sick man again and clothed him.

---

[151] This means that it was a house attached to some settled religious order, not a house of Franciscans.
(author note)

This "simple" approach to living a Christian life was revolutionary because it used the Gospel, on a literal level, as a model of life. Francis viewed himself and his followers as apostles, in the way that the 70 whom Jesus sent out to spread the Gospel were apostles during the lifetime of Jesus.[152] They were allowed only one tunic, but no cloak or coat. They were allowed no established place to live, for the Son of Man had no place to rest His head.[153] They were not allowed to judge others (and Francis took this command to the ultimate extreme). They were allowed no property, not even strictly religious property. In order to see how these guidelines controlled the lives of the friars we should look at three stories:[154]

> Along about the year 1213, Brother Angelo Tarlati, who like his namesake Angelo Tancredi, was a former knight, was living at the hermitage of Monte Casale. As porter, he one day received a visit from three notorious robbers who, lacking travelers to rob in the neighboring woods, had come to the convent to beg alms. He gave them a very poor reception:
> "What? Murderers like you? Not satisfied with robbing honest folk of the fruit of their toil, you want to take the little belonging to God's servants! You, who have no respect for God or man don't deserve that the earth

---

[152] See *Matthew* 10, *Mark* 6, *Luke* 9 + 10
[153] For example, *Matthew* 8:20
[154] Englebert, 92-93; Englebert, 97; Englebert, 208.

should hold you! Get out of here, and don't let me see you again!"

Perhaps the fiery guardian called on his sword which in former days he used to thrust through rascals like them. Be that as it may, the robbers withdrew in high anger. But scarcely had they left when Francis returned, laden down with the bread and wine which he had collected as alms. Learning what had happened, he reproached the porter:

"You have behaved like a man with no religion!" he said. "Does not the Gospel which we have promised to follow declare that it is the sick and not the well who need a doctor? Take this bread and this wine in the name of obedience, and go and find those robbers! Run up hill and down dale until you find them; and as soon as you see them, shout, 'Come, brother robbers! Come and eat the good things Brother Francis begs you to accept!'

"And they will come. Then spread a cloth on the ground and put this bread and this wine on it, to which you will add some eggs and cheese. And serve these unfortunate men with humility and good humor until they are satisfied. Then, and not until then, ask them not to kill anybody anymore, adding that serving God is not nearly so hard as their profession. And I do not doubt the Lord in His mercy will inspire them with better sentiments."

Nor was their conversion long delayed. For from this time on, says the chronicler, they were to be seen every day at the hermitage, bringing on their backs the firewood needed by the friars. And not only did they pledge themselves to gain their living from then on by honest toil, but all three ended up by entering the Order, in which they died the death of saints.

After the death of St. Francis, Juniper's charity took a special turn, and the idea often came to him of distributing to the poor the books and other objects that he deemed superfluous in the Franciscan House. The friars had to put the things under lock and key or else have them disappear.

Now how was it, with a reputation like that, that Juniper was entrusted on a feast day with the care of the altar of the Basilica of Assisi? The fact remains that he profited by his charge to detach some costly silver ringlets from the altar frontal and give them to a beggar woman. Furious, the Minister General[155] stormed so at Juniper that he almost lost his voice. That night, hearing a knock at the door, he opened it to see Brother Juniper standing there with a candle in one hand and a dish in the other.

---

[155] The Minister General is the head of the Order of Friars Minor. This was not just anyone that Juniper was upsetting.

"Father", said he, "you shouted so a while ago that I thought you must be hoarse. So I've brought you some buttered gruel which will do your throat and chest a lot of good."

The superior refused the remedy and curtly invited Juniper to stop his silly pranks.

"Very well", replied Juniper. "Since you scorn my gruel, which was not made to be thrown away, then please hold a candle for me, and I'll eat it."

Before such simplicity, the Minister was disarmed, and the two religious feasted fraternally together.

As this novice had been authorized by Elias to have a psalter, he came to Francis to have the permission confirmed. "Once you have a psalter", replied Francis, "you will want a breviary. And when you have a breviary, no longer deigning to disturb yourself, you will say haughtily to your brother, 'Brother, please fetch my breviary!'" Then taking up a handful of ashes, he began to rub his head with them, saying: "I-a breviary! I-a breviary!"

(That is a wonderfully vivid acting-out on the part of Francis of the idea that the smallest kind of possession leads inevitably to a tendency to make much of ourselves and to sin with pride. It is a very biblical moment, when Francis rubs his head with ashes like Job in his lamenting. This shows clearly that Francis used acting to teach those inside the Order as well as those outside, among the public.)

What is the point of all of these stories? Do they add up to anything more than just some picturesque snapshots from the Christian past?

Well, to begin with, Christians of the time of Francis lived in a more hierarchical and mutually connected society than we do. In order for people to withdraw from it, they needed to be direct and decisive to cut the cords that bound them to other people. They were stepping not only out of the world but out of their very concretely established places in society and that was a difficult thing to do for their society was made of very sticky stuff.

Francis was convinced that each attachment leads to other attachments. That is why he was so set on arranging every little detail of the life of his Order in a way to minimize these attachments. "Sisters", even spiritual sisters, are family and family is something that Christians have been instructed to put behind them. "Ladies" are not so threatening to the Christian calling for a man because, in the knightly culture of the Middle Ages, ladies are people that one can honorably serve as a part of one's religious practice. (Knightly life was considered a religious calling, we must remember.) The obligations men have toward family members, on the other hand, are not voluntary. They are an inescapable part of that relationship and are forced on us by society. But, the obligations men have of knightly service toward ladies are voluntary and separate from the demands of the practical world around them. In that way, they are not chains that bind us, but chances to show the quality of our new life, Francis thought.

This is a very interesting and characteristic example of Francis's imaginative use of the latent potential of his culture for Christian reworking. In the same way that the western Church tried to rework the Germanic fascination with warfare into a force for Christian good, Francis tried to rework the knightly urge into a further spur for his followers toward selfless Christian service. In our own culture, we would need to approach the matter of finding useful links with the Gospel from a very different starting point, but Francis's example is worthy of great respect and has much to teach us. St. Paul would recognize that his own experience of being "made all things to all men"[156] found an echo in Francis's Christian knighthood. It is not surprising that early sources about Francis show that more than one knight joined the followers of Francis to live out his calling there. (Remember that Br. Angelo was the one who had to run after the robbers to serve them a picnic. That was surely a very different way of being a knight than he was used to!)

Let us return to Francis's idea that detachment from the world is necessary for a full connection to Jesus Christ. Jesus Christ says that we must choose Him before family, and this idea that the natural attachment to family was something that must be avoided was very strong among the earliest Franciscans. Listen to this brief story about Brother Giles, whom many consider to be the purest example of the early Franciscan:[157]

> When Brother Giles once came to Assisi, the friars took him round their new home, showing him the splendid buildings which they had put up, and apparently taking great pride in them. But when Brother Giles had carefully looked at them all, he said to the

---

[156] *1 Corinthians* 9:22
[157] ANF, 29

brethren: "You know, brethren, there is only one thing you're short of now, and that's *wives*!" The brothers were deeply shocked at this; so Brother Giles said to them: "My brothers, you know well enough that it is just as illegal[158] for you to give up Poverty as to give up Chastity. After throwing Poverty overboard it is easy enough to throw Chastity as well."

Here, we can see that giving up the things of the world is understood among the Franciscans to be a single, seamless whole. If we are going to deny ourselves one part of a normal life on earth we must deny ourselves all of it or, one by one, the elements of the normal human life will creep back in and we will find ourselves living back in the world again. Simplicity, because it does not allow one to make fine distinctions or to imagine subtle shadings in matters that should be black and white, was a great protection to the integrity with which Francis tried to live his life. This made it an important element in the success of Francis's dedication to his new style of life.

St. Francis's experience of trying to find the space he needed to live out his vocation showed him that he did not only need to steer clear of the more worldly of the people who surrounded him but of the religious ones, as well. One of my favorite stories about St. Francis is a good example of the way in which the instincts of the world, even the best religious instincts of the world, work

---

[158] Here, "illegal" means "against the Rule that Francis had written for the Order". (author's note)

almost in the opposite direction from the instincts of St. Francis. What is particularly interesting, to me, about this story, which is told by St. Bonaventure in one of his letters but does not appear in his life of Francis, is that I think that St. Bonaventure has misunderstood it. If I am right, then those who misunderstood Francis included some who were closest to him and sought to follow him with the most sincerity.[159]

> In order that you may know how much Saint Francis approved of Bible-reading, let me tell you what I heard from a certain friar. He told me that when a copy of the New Testament was given to the brethren, and since it was impossible for them all to read it at once, Saint Francis divided it up into single sheets and gave one page to each brother, in order that all might study it and none interfere with another.

St. Bonaventure says he thinks that this story is an example of St. Francis's desire for all the brethren to be able to read the New Testament as much as possible. I do not think that that is correct. I think that what we have, here, is an example of St. Francis's desire to distance himself and his followers from the normal scale of values of the world and, at the same time, to honor the gift that the brethren had been given. We need to remember that books, during the Middle Ages, were among the most expensive objects that existed in Europe. I am always amazed when

---

[159] ANF, 60

I see a medieval manuscript with a gold cover that is festooned with jewels, but it is important to remember that, at the time that the cover was produced, the inside pages were more valuable than the cover that was put on them. The education, training, and labor involved in producing a Bible or New Testament was immense. For someone to give such an object to the brethren was an extravagant act of charity on a par with giving them golden vessels to have on their altar.

We have already seen stories about how the vessels on the altar were given away by followers of Francis to help the poor, so we know what he might have decided to do with that sort of gift. Francis, however, could not just give the New Testament away to anyone who was in need. We know from many stories that Francis had a great reverence for any object that might have the name of God written on it, so he would have been very careful about whom he gave a Bible to.[160] He knew that the members of the Brotherhood were very reverent and would treat the New Testament with respect, so he could give the pages of the New Testament to them with a clear conscience. He could rid the Order of this troublesome piece of wealth while also treating it as a precious gift worthy of reverence if he handed it out in single sheets to be kept like little relics by the brothers, most of whom would not have been able to read it, anyway.

I think his handing out the New Testament page by page to the brethren was not a sign of his valuing study, but rather a sign of his devaluing study and the hierarchy it brings. Instead of the few literate brothers being a

---

[160] See Richest, 54-55 for some characteristic examples.

special, insider group who would be allowed access to the precious New Testament now owned by the Order, all the brethren could have an equal piece and could hold the folded page, which had the names of Jesus and of God written on it, close to their hearts inside their robes. It seems to me to be a perfect Franciscan solution to a potentially difficult problem. It makes just the right kind of nonsensical sense for Francis to have acted that way. I think that, by doing this, he wanted to make clear to his followers that they were called to treat the physical things of the world in a very different way than the general run of people were. (I hardly need to tell you that St. Jerome, not St. Francis, is the patron saint of librarians.)

There is a practical aspect to Francis's approach to following Jesus that we should not overlook. It has to do with the usual Christian idea of what advancement in holiness is thought to offer those who achieve it. Like all Christians before him, and after him, Francis was convinced that further progress in the Christian life would lead him to a clearer understanding of what Christian life should be. Given that assumption, his emphasis on following the clear commands of Jesus makes even more sense. If we do not follow the clear commands we are given, how will we develop the discernment to understand the less clear ones? How can we hope to make progress in the Christian life and come to greater understanding if we do not take the first, most obvious baby steps? Francis trusted the Holy Ghost to lead him into all truth[161] if he showed himself willing to do what he was told and so to be worthy of further grace. His willingness, when led by

---

[161] *John* 16:13

the Holy Ghost, to do things he would never otherwise do would be the evidence of his dependence on God and his openness to grace.

Francis sought to remake his life entirely in Jesus' image. He began with the most obvious things and trusted that the later steps in the process would get clearer and easier as he went along. This was not an easy way of life. Even Francis found it hard to make himself live the life he felt called to live. We hear of Francis taking off his one tunic in the coldest part of the winter and letting the wind play over his naked body, so that when he put his single tunic back on again, it would seem warmer than it had before.[162] His life involved great suffering, at times. He found it very difficult, in the most mundane and practical way, to follow the clear instructions of Jesus. Still, he trusted that if he did so, he would come to a greater understanding of them and would progress in the Christian life to a stage where things would become easier. The simplicity with which he tried to approach Christian living was intended by Francis to be both a sign of his humility and also a first, obvious step on the way to a greater understanding of God and a greater closeness with Jesus.

Francis did not disdain the most obvious steps in trying to liken his life to the life led by Jesus in the gospels. In some ways, this willingness to do the most mundane things was the "simplest" thing about his vision. He started with the most immediate and obvious things and went on from there. For all his unusual appearance,

---

[162] See Biography, 35 where the tale is discussed, and ANF, 42 (sec. 30) where the story is recounted.

Francis was looking for the shortest route to Jesus, so he thought through how that should be done and began doing the things he thought he ought to do, one by one. (The moment in the movie version of *The Wizard of Oz* when Glinda the Good Witch makes Judy Garland go back to the very beginning of that curly yellow spiral of bricks that begins the Yellow Brick Road always reminds me of Francis. He would have approved of Glinda's insistence that the best way to start is to go all the way to the beginning and to pick up there.) Francis did not want to be a Christian in a new way that no one had ever thought of, he wanted to be a Christian so he could be close to Jesus Christ. There is a lesson here for anyone who wants to be a better Christian: doing the obvious thing is not less valuable than doing something obscure that no one ever thought of, and it may be better: at least, with the obvious thing, you know that it is something God wants. That is what St. Francis thought.

> O God, who for our redemption didst give thine only-begotten Son to the death of the Cross, and by his glorious resurrection hast delivered us from the power of our enemy; Grant us so to die daily from sin, that we may evermore live with him in the joy of his resurrection; through the same thy Son Christ our Lord. *Amen.*[163]

---

[163] BCP, 165

Chapter 16

LOVE OF POVERTY

> Almighty God, whose loving hand hath given us all that we possess; Grant us grace that we may honour thee with our substance, and remembering the account which we must one day give, may be faithful stewards of thy bounty; through Jesus Christ our Lord. *Amen.*[164]

In some ways, the love of poverty was the most characteristic of Francis's emphases, because it allowed him to separate from the world, which was one of the most basic goals toward which his practices were aimed. As Bishop Moorman puts it so clearly:[165]

> Once Francis had accepted poverty as an ideal, he began to clothe it with the language of imagination and romance. To be destitute was to cast oneself upon God, to depend on him as a small child depends upon its parents for everything. While other men were tied down by the burden of making a living, Francis was free to enjoy what God gave him.

This sounds very odd to us, in our mercantile culture, to think of poverty as freedom instead of as a prison, but

---

[164] BCP, 599
[165] Richest, 82-83

it tallies very well with Francis's upside-down view of the practicalities of life.

It may not surprise us to discover that, in real life rather than in a book, this upside-downness of Francis's thinking could be hard to put up with, sometimes, even for those who loved him best and followed him most closely. It is interesting, also, that his followers told stories that illustrated their exasperation with Francis very vividly. They did not try to hide this feeling. (In that, Francis is like Jesus, Whose followers often found Him beyond their comprehension.) Here is a famous example that makes clear how Francis thought of poverty and the effect that poverty had on his life.

In *The Little Flowers* there is a story in which Brother Masseo is upset with Francis when they have collected a few crusts at the end of the day and Francis looks at them with rapture and calls them "great treasure". We might well feel, as we read the story, that Brother Masseo has a point and that we might have said the same thing he did, especially if we had gone through a hard day that was topped off by wearying begging, as those two had. Francis's reply, however, is quite consistent with his usual views. Masseo says:[166]

> 'Father, how can this be called treasure, when we are in such poverty, and lack the things of which we have need; we, who have neither cloth, nor knives, nor plates, nor bowl, nor house, nor table, nor manservant nor maidservant?' Then said St. Francis: 'This

---

[166] *The Little Flowers*, 13, quoted at Richest, 84

is what I call a great treasure, that there is nothing here provided by human industry, but everything is provided by Divine Providence, as we may see manifestly in this bread which we have begged, in the stone which serves so beautifully for our table, and in this so clear fountain; and therefore I desire that we should pray to God that He would cause holy poverty, which is a thing so noble that God himself was made subject to it, to be loved by us with our whole heart.' And when he had said these words, and they had made their prayer, and partaken for bodily refreshment of the pieces of bread, and drunk of the water, they arose and went on their way.

I hope you noticed, by the way, that St. Francis declared that poverty was such a wonderful thing "that God himself was made subject to it". That is, Francis made clear that he believed that Jesus Himself had lived a life of poverty. It is not really important, for our purposes, that Francis's idea about Jesus' life of voluntary poverty seems to be incorrect. What is important for us to realize is that Francis's desire to separate from the world through poverty is a part of his desire to imitate what he saw of the life of Christ in the Gospels.

There was more than just an attempt to imitate Jesus motivating Francis's poverty, though. In an odd way, it allowed him to achieve one of his old, pre-conversion dreams. Poverty allowed Francis to continue in knightly service, which had always been one of his deepest desires. Now, of course, his knightly service was offered to Lady Poverty herself and to the Virgin Mary, instead of to an earthly lady, but it was heart-felt, voluntary service with no thought of any reward, nonetheless. (There is a level on which Don Quixote shares a piece of Francis's vision, which, I think, is why Cervantes' novel is more than just a comedy.)

Poverty allowed Francis to welcome other people into his life.

Poverty allowed Francis and his followers a way of acting out their penitence.

Poverty provided opportunities for charitable action to people beyond the bounds of the Order itself.[167]

Because modern Americans live lives of such abundance and physical comfort, we tend to focus on the physical privations involved in Francis's interest in poverty instead of on his motives in pursuing poverty, in the first place. It is a mistake, however, for us to think that everything he did that involved giving things away was, therefore, motivated by his desire for poverty. For example, Francis's most famous act of renunciation: that of giving up all he had received from his father, Peter Bernadone, in order to be completely free from him, was not, in itself, really intended as an act of poverty. More than a renunciation of his property, it was a renunciation of his human family so that Francis could be God's child, and His alone, instead of the child of a human father. This is a tremendously important point. It shows that poverty was not, strictly speaking, an end in itself, for Francis, but rather was a means to Francis's greater end of cleaving more closely to God. Let us look again at this scene of Francis's great renunciation as St. Bonaventure presents it.[168]

---

[167] See Richest, 89

[168] Bonaventure, 2.4, 17

Thereupon his carnally minded father led this child of grace, now stripped of his money, before the bishop of the town. He wanted to have Francis renounce into his hands his family possessions and return everything he had. A true lover of poverty, Francis showed himself eager to comply; he went before the bishop without delaying or hesitating. He did not wait for any words nor did he speak any, but immediately took off his clothes and gave them back to his father. Then it was discovered that the man of God had a hairshirt next to his skin under his fine clothes. Moreover, drunk with remarkable fervor, he even took off his underwear, stripping himself completely naked before all. He said to his father: "Until now I have called you father here on earth, but now I can say without reservation, 'Our Father who art in heaven' (Matt. 6:9), since I have placed all my treasure and all my hope in him."[169] When the bishop saw this, he was amazed at such intense fervor in the man of God. He immediately stood up and in tears drew Francis into his arms, covering him with the mantle he was wearing, like the pious and good man that he was. He bade his servants give Francis something to cover his body. They brought him a poor, cheap cloak

---

[169] This is clearly a reference both to Francis's having given away a lot of his father's goods in charity and to Jesus' teaching in the Sermon on the Mount about laying up our treasure in Heaven instead of on earth. [Matt. 6:19-21] (author's note)

of a farmer who worked for the bishop. Francis accepted it gratefully and with his own hand marked a cross on it with a piece of chalk, thus designating it as the covering of a crucified man and a half-naked beggar.

In a society in which people marked their status and identity through the clothing they wore, Francis's taking off his fancy Bernadone clothing and putting on the poor clothing given him in charity, and especially his marking it with a cross (very much in the manner of a knight putting his coat of arms on his shield, especially of a crusader wearing the Cross over his usual badge), was an extravagant public expression of his new allegiance to God alone and his separation from his old earthly allegiances.

That is an important point, in itself. Francis's poverty was not just a negative, it was not just giving things up, it was also a positive action.[170] Poverty was a way to draw closer to Jesus; poverty was Lady Poverty, a mistress to be served. Poverty was the symbol and substance of the new life that Francis was convinced would bring him closer to God. Look at this description from St. Bonaventure's life of Francis.[171]

Among the gifts of grace which Francis received from God the generous Giver, he merited as a special privilege to grow in the riches of simplicity through his love of the highest poverty. The holy man saw that poverty was a close companion of the Son of God, and now

---

[170] See Biography, 33
[171] Bonventure, 7.1, 67-68

that it was rejected by the whole world, he was eager to espouse it in everlasting love. For the sake of poverty he not only left his father and mother, but also gave away everything he had. No one was so greedy for gold as he was for poverty; nor was anyone so anxious to guard his treasure as he was in guarding this pearl of the Gospel. In this especially would his sight be offended if he saw in the friars anything which did not accord completely with poverty. Indeed, from the beginning of his religious life until his death, his only riches were a tunic, a cord and underclothes; and with this much he was content. He used to frequently call to mind with tears the poverty of Jesus Christ and his mother, claiming that it was the queen of the virtues because it shone forth so preeminently in the King of Kings and the Queen, his mother.

Bonaventure's choice of words in this passage is very careful. He says that Francis "was eager to espouse [poverty] in everlasting love". That is literally true. Francis was wooing poverty as a courtly lover would woo the lady he wished to marry. This is one of the chief ways in which Francis sought to combine a courtly, knightly life of service with his life of religious service to God and the Virgin Mary. St. Francis was in love with the life he led and one of the places in which he expressed that love most clearly was in his discussions of poverty. It is entirely fitting that the earliest piece of writing about St. Francis is an allegory about his wooing and marrying Lady Poverty, the lady whom all others neglect.[172]

---

[172] History, 278-279. This writing, "Francis and His Lady Poverty", can be found, with introduction, at Habig, 1531-1596.

Our earlier discussion of Francis's stripping himself of his clothes before the bishop of Assisi should remind us of one of the central benefits of the Order's emphasis on poverty. The story we looked at in the last chapter in which Francis was insistent that the brothers own neither Psalters nor Breviaries, because having them would lead them to lord it over each other, should give us a clear indication of how poverty could be connected to rank, even rank within the Order itself. Owning things means noticing distinctions between people based on what they own. Also, many of the most conspicuous and valuable possessions in their society related to war, something Francis had put behind him and insisted that all his followers should avoid, too. (This was, and still is, standard practice for members of religious orders.) In a society in which one of the most prominent and dominant ranks was the one occupied by warriors, poverty was also useful in keeping the brothers away from that whole side of life. The friars not only had nothing to fight **for**, they also had nothing to fight **with**, which denied them many of the roles commonly coveted in their society.

Despite the fact that there were many monastic houses in Europe during Francis's life and that the idea of giving up all property for a religious calling was well established in people's minds, it is a constant theme in our material about Francis that many people thought he was trying to be **too** poor. Francis's explanation of why he approaches poverty in such an aggressive way is expressed well in a conversation he is reported to have had with the bishop of Assisi. Like many of the people who admired Francis the most and had his well-being closest to their hearts, the bishop of Assisi was very concerned about the fervor and stringency of Francis's approach to poverty.

One day, he is reported to have addressed St. Francis on just this topic: [173]

> 'It seems to me', he said, 'that it is very hard and difficult to possess nothing in the world.' To this blessed Francis replied: 'My lord, if we had any possessions we should also be forced to have arms to protect them, since possessions are a cause of disputes and strife, and in many ways we should be hindered from loving God and our neighbors. Therefore in this life we wish to have no temporal possessions'. The Bishop was greatly pleased by these words of God's servant; and indeed Francis despised all passing things, especially money, so much that he laid the greatest stress on holy poverty and insisted that the brothers should be most careful to avoid money.

It is important for us to realize, as we look at Francis's teaching on poverty, that it was the source of many difficulties for him throughout the course of his religious life. As his public life went on and his notoriety increased, the details of these difficulties changed but all of his poverty-related problems stemmed either from the practical needs of the men for survival, brought to the fore by the momentum of the huge movement Francis had sparked, or from the desire of many outside the Order to put this energetic body of men to good use.

Francis's attempts to cling to poverty for his Order took many forms. For example, he did everything he

---

[173] Richest, 87

could to resist having special places for himself and his followers to live. In their age, as well as in ours, real-estate was one of the most important, and expensive, forms of property and it proved to be one of the most difficult forms of property for the Order to avoid. Among the most vivid examples of his frustration with this struggle are the stories told about Francis's arrival in Bologna to visit the community of friars there only to discover that they were living in a house that had been specially built for them. He refused to go inside the building at all and ordered all the friars living there to leave immediately, including the sick, which proved to be a very difficult thing for the brothers to do and a very difficult thing for the brothers and the pious in Bologna to understand.[174] There are, also, the stories told of Francis's return to the little chapel of the Portiuncula in the plain below Assisi, which was perhaps his favorite place on earth, to discover that a building had been constucted there out of stone and mortar for the friars to live in. Francis immediately climbed up on the roof and began pulling the building to pieces and throwing the pieces off the roof, until he was told that the building belonged to the city of Assisi and not to the friars, which made him stop and climb down so he would not be guilty of destroying someone else's property.[175]

That is a very good example of the kind of difficulties Francis had in controlling his Order that sprang directly from the enthusiasm of people outside the Order for what St. Francis was trying to do. As one reads about Francis's life, it often seems that, the more people revered

---

[174] See Richest, 89
[175] See Richest, 89

Francis, the more they got in the way of what he was actually trying to do. This is the clearest possible evidence of how out of the ordinary his aims were, since, even those who desired to support him almost always ended by getting in his way, instead. A good example of this is the story told of Francis arriving at a Franciscan friary for Christmas and being so taken aback by the splendid nature of the meal they set out for him for the feast that he went outside again and tried to disguise himself and then knocked at the door as a beggar, to try to show the brothers that they were living more richly than friars should.[176] Of course his trick did not work: they knew right away who it was, so when Francis sat down to eat his meal on the floor, disdaining to use the table, he spoke to them, openly, as their founder:

> When I saw the table elaborately and carefully laid, I felt that this was not the table of poor religious who go around for alms from door to door each day. Dearest brothers, we are under a greater obligation than other religious to follow the example of Christ's humility and poverty, for it is to this end that we have been called and professed before God and men. So it seems to me that it is I who am sitting like a Friar Minor, because the feasts of our Lord and the Saints are better honoured in the want and poverty by which these Saints won heaven, than in the luxury

---

[176] Richest, 91

and excess by which a soul is estranged from heaven.

Francis's vision and teaching is clear, but his Order was not taking them as its guide. It is easy to see that, though his followers felt great reverence for him, Francis could no longer really direct the way they lived their lives.

An even better example of Francis's difficulties in following his vocation because of the piety of the Christians around him can be found in the story of his dinner at the house of the Bishop of Ostia in Rome. As you read this story, pay attention to how those around Francis respond to what he is doing. It is clear that, on one level, they understand something of his actions and intentions, because they seem to recognize them as springing from a truly Christian desire, but do they take them in the way that Francis intends? The difficulty that he confronts in this situation springs from the fact that Francis is still trying to be a good servant of Lady Poverty while he is also a guest at the luxurious table of the bishop. In other words, it comes from the awkward juxtaposition of his unworldliness with his attempt to live his life as a witness to the world around him. [177]

> ...he went out for alms, and returning placed some of the scraps of black bread on the bishop's table. When the bishop saw this he was somewhat ashamed, above all because of the newly invited guests. The father, how-

---

[177] Richest, 92

ever, with a joyous countenance distributed the alms which he had received to the knights and chaplains gathered about the table. All of them accepted the alms with wonderful devotion and some of them ate them, others kept them out of reverence. When the dinner was finished, the bishop arose; and, taking the man of God to an inner room, he raised his arms and embraced him. 'My brother,' he said, 'why did you bring shame on me in the house that is yours and your brothers, by going out for alms?' The saint said to him: 'Rather I have shown you honour, for I have honoured a greater lord. For the Lord is well pleased with poverty, and above all with that poverty that is voluntary. For I have a royal dignity and a special nobility, namely, to follow the Lord who, being rich, became poor for us.' And he added: 'I get more light from a poor table that is furnished with small alms than from great tables on which dainty foods are placed almost without number.' Then, greatly edified, the bishop said to the saint: 'Son, do what seems good in your eyes, for the Lord is with you.'

Everyone in this story seems greatly 'edified' by having Francis among them. They are very glad that he acts so much in character. Some of them even keep the little crusts of bread that he had begged as relics of their meeting with him. But, for all their being 'edified', none of them seems to be particularly changed by this encounter. Rather than showing the success of Francis in spreading his idea of poverty, this incident actually shows that many of the problems that prevented Francis from accomplishing what he felt called to do stemmed, in later years, from people's reverence for him rather than the hostility that had afflicted the little group at the start. After all, it is because of people's reverence that he was invited to dinner at the bishop's table in the first place, and it was because of their reverence for him that they did not view his actions among them as a challenge to their faith but, instead, as a wonderful 'Francis story' that they could tell for the rest of their lives.

The more the surrounding society revered Francis, the more he could not follow his vocation. His giving up the headship of the Order in 1220 was a sign that it had passed beyond him and become something he had never wanted. The great basilica at the Portiuncula, where the original little chapel has been made a relic, and the greater, double basilica in Assisi, with the beautiful Giotto frescoes on the walls[178], where his body lies, manage to be both acts of veneration toward Francis and acts of repudiation of all that he was trying to be, himself, and trying to teach the world to be, through his works. The visitor to Assisi with some knowledge of Francis's life and teaching cannot help marveling at how so much reverence for him can be accompanied by such a complete lack of appreciation for what he was trying to do and to inspire others to do.

Probably, the movement's size made the changes unavoidable, in the time and place these things happened. It is important to remember, too, lest we fall into blaming all lovers of Francis for their shortcomings without

[178] These can be seen, beautifully photographed, at www.http:// gallery.euroweb.hu/html/g/giotto/assisi

acknowledging their many virtues, that our memory of Francis' original desires and of the anger felt by him and some of his early followers at the changes in the Order are available to us only because the Order, itself, preserved them. The Church always treated the spiritual Franciscans[179] with great forbearance and respect and we should remember that fact, even as we look at just a few stories that, whether they are true or not, show very vividly the anger and frustration felt by some early Franciscans at the Order's turning its back on Francis's vision of the life of poverty. Before we do, I would like to just remind you of the story of brother Giles telling the Franciscans who were living in a fine stone building that all they had left to do was to get wives, now that they had given up poverty. That story seems to be a true one and rings with a real Franciscan voice.

Here is a story that I am certain is **not** historical (since Francis would never have cursed anyone and, if he had, Jesus would never have approved that curse and given it power), but the story is certainly a very good indication of the feelings of anger sparked in many by this change in the Order.[180]

A certain Friar Minor, Brother John of Sciaca, was minister[181] of Bologna in the time

---

[179] The order suffered from upsets and splits for almost three centuries after Francis's death. During that time, the most usual term for those who held to a more rigorous pursuit of Francis's example was "spiritual Franciscans". Bp. Moorman's history of the Order up to 1517 is the obvious first place to go for more information on this topic.

[180] ANF, 37-38. We have seen enough to realize that the spiritual Franciscans thought that their brethren in Bologna were a very troublesome group.

[181] That means that he was the head of the Friars Minor in Bologna. (author's note)

of Saint Francis, and a very learned man who, without leave from the Saint, founded a place of study at Bologna. When Francis heard of this he went at once to Bologna and sharply reproved the minister, saying: "You are trying to destroy my order! After the manner of Christ Jesus I have always wanted my friars to pray rather than to read." And when he was going away from Bologna, Francis cursed the minister with a mighty curse. Then the minister began to be ill, and, as his sickness increased, he sent by the brothers for Saint Francis to ask him to revoke his malediction. The Saint replied: "That curse which I put upon him has been ratified in heaven by the Lord Jesus". So the poor minister lay in misery on his bed, with little consolation. And suddenly one day there came from heaven a ball of fire and sulphur which smote right through his body and the bed on which he was lying; and, with a foul stench, the wretched man expired and the devil received his soul.

Well, that certainly shows that there were members of the Order who thought that all the "developments" and "coming to maturity" that had occurred in the Order were nothing less than treason against Francis and his memory. By telling this story, they were trying to enlist Francis's memory and reputation in their struggle against the Order of the Friars Minor turning into a rich and powerful international organization, which it very quickly did.

Here is another story, from a different source, that shows the great concern felt among the early Franciscans at the rise of study and scholarship in the Order. We have already seen Francis's treatment of books in that story where he pulled apart the New Testament into its individual pages. In this story, we can see what one of Francis's most famous companions thought of learning.[182]

> The holy Brother Conrad once heard from Brother Leo, the companion of Saint Francis, that he (Brother Leo) woke one night in a great fright and went to say Mattins with the Blessed Francis. And he told the Saint that he had had a most alarming dream. And Saint Francis said to him: "What did you dream?" And he said: "I seemed to be standing close to a stream, white and foaming, and many friars came to cross over, and since they were carrying books in their hands, they perished in the flood. And I also, when I wanted to cross, was holding a Breviary, and I should have been drowned in the water. So I threw the book away because otherwise I could not have crossed. Then I got over..." Then the Blessed Francis answered with pain and grief: "O Brother Leo, these books are bad and will ruin the Order. I would not allow anyone to become a Friar Minor unless he is content with being able to say the 'Our Father'."

---

[182] ANF, 38-39

That tale rings with the true voice of Francis, but shows that he knew that his wishes were not being followed. Francis sought a simple, dedicated group of men to pray and preach and help the poor, but he produced a very different thing, in the end. Instead of gathering men who only wanted to pray the Lord's Prayer and rest content, Francis's Order quickly produced St. Bonaventure, who was the last great Platonist theologian in the Latin Church, as well as generations of energetic academics who reinvigorated the universities of Europe and founded many new schools of all sorts that survive to the present day. Good things came out of Francis's life and work, but they were not the good things he aimed to produce.

For the whole course of his life, Francis stood firmly against the human desire to acquire things and to complicate and elaborate the things we do. He was convinced that the truest Christian life is the life devoted, not to the things of this world, but to the Creator of this world. While his vision could excite many people outside the Order and inspire them to pious thoughts and, often, pious actions, he never could get them to appreciate fully or even to understand what he was trying to do.

> O most loving Father, who willest us to give thanks for all things, to dread nothing but the loss of thee, and to cast all our care on thee, who carest for us; Preserve us from faithless fears and worldly anxieties, and grant that no clouds of this mortal life may hide from us the light of that love which is immortal, and which thou hast manifested unto us in thy Son, Jesus Christ our Lord. *Amen.*[183]

---

[183] BCP, 596

Chapter 17

SERMON AT SUNDAY SERVICE
Sermon text: *Matthew* 10:1-24

And when he had called unto him his
twelve disciples, he gave them power
against unclean spirits, to cast them out,
and to heal all manner of sickness and
all manner of disease.
Now the names of the twelve apostles
are these; The first, Simon, who is called
Peter, and Andrew his brother; James the
son of
Zebedee, and John his brother;
Philip, and Bartholomew; Thomas, and
Matthew the publican;
James the son of Alphaeus, and
Lebbaeus, whose surname was
Thaddaeus;
Simon the Canaanite, and Judas Iscariot,
who also betrayed him.
These twelve Jesus sent forth, and
commanded them, saying, Go not into
the way of the Gentiles, and into any
city of the Samaritans enter ye not:
But go rather to the lost sheep of the
house of Israel.
And as ye go, preach, saying, The
kingdom of heaven is at hand.
Heal the sick, cleanse the lepers, raise

the dead, cast out devils: freely ye have
received, freely give.
Provide neither gold, nor silver, nor
brass in your purses,
Nor scrip for your journey, neither two
coats, neither shoes, nor yet staves: for
the workman is worthy of his meat.
And into whatsoever city or town ye
shall enter, enquire who in it is worthy;
and there abide till ye go thence.
And when ye come into an house, salute
it.
And if the house be worthy, let your
peace come upon it: but if it be not
worthy, let your peace return to you.
And whosoever shall not receive you,
nor hear your words, when ye depart out
of that house or city, shake off the dust
of your feet.
Verily I say unto you, It shall be more
tolerable for the land of
Sodom and Gomorrha in the day of
judgment, than for that city.
Behold, I send you forth as sheep in the
midst of wolves: be ye therefore wise as
serpents, and harmless as doves.
But beware of men: for they will deliver
you up to the councils, and they will
scourge you in their synagogues;
And ye shall be brought before
governors and kings for my sake, for

a testimony against them and the
Gentiles.

But when they deliver you up, take no
thought how or what ye shall speak: for
it shall be given you in that same hour
what ye shall speak.

For it is not ye that speak, but the Spirit
of your Father which speaketh in you.

And the brother shall deliver up the
brother to death, and the father the
child: and the children shall rise up
against their parents, and cause them to
be put to death.

And ye shall be hated of all men for my
name's sake: but he that endureth to the
end shall be saved.

But when they persecute you in this city,
flee ye into another: for verily I say unto
you, Ye shall not have gone over the
cities of

Israel, till the Son of man be come.

The disciple is not above his master, nor
the servant above his

Lord.

We do not know exactly what scriptural passage it
was that spurred St. Francis to leave his individual hermit's life and embark on a public career in the Church,
but there is enough information in the early accounts of
his life for us to know that it was one of the missionary
passages. Under the influence of hearing a passage just

like the tenth chapter of St. Matthew's gospel, St. Francis changed his focus from the interior to the exterior and changed from being a hermit to being a herald. The influence of a passage like this is evident in the fact that it was only after he had gathered 11 followers together that Francis ventured to take his rule to Rome for the approval of the pope. Chapter 3 of St. Bonaventure's life of St. Francis recounts this for us.[184] Francis was trying to reenact the first going out into the world of Christ's disciples during His ministry. This is another indication of the dedication Francis exercised in trying to model his life on the life we see lived by Christians in the Gospels.[185] Because we know that these passages spurred Francis to

---

[184] 3.7 + 8, 28 and following, show this process very clearly.

[185] Sometimes it is said that Francis was trying to be Jesus. While it is true that Francis wanted to imitate Christ in his behavior, which is the oldest way of describing the attempt to live a serious Christian life (see Phil. 2:5-13), he would never have presumed to liken himself to Jesus. Francis always numbered himself among the followers of Jesus when he was trying to recreate the gospel life. His waiting until he had 11 companions before he ventured to Rome to ask for the Pope's blessing is the clearest evidence of this. Francis not only did not want to be Jesus, he also did not want to be Peter (as his reluctance to serve as ruler over his Order shows). If Francis could have chosen a Disciple to emulate, he would surely have chosen one of those whose name alone is known to us. To think of Francis as living his life in the hopes of being another Bartholomew is truer to his vision than to saddle him with dreams of glory and importance that he gave up completely at his conversion. Francis did not turn from seeking earthly glory as a knight to seeking churchly glory as a leader of men. He turned from seeking earthly glory to seeking to live the most inglorious life possible. If we do not see this clearly, we cannot see Francis clearly.

change his life, I think it makes sense to use this passage from *The Gospel according to St. Matthew* to try to get an idea of the situation Francis was trying to recreate in the rules he set up for his Order and in his own life.

The first thing we see in this passage is that Jesus allows no cushion for the convenience of the apostles. They exercise their ministry and live their lives completely exposed to the vagaries of living as wanderers in the world. Everything they do is undertaken in an atmosphere of estrangement, if not hostility, between the followers of Jesus and the world around them. There is no promise of success offered to even the most dedicated and single-minded apostle. As a matter of fact, we can see in this passage[186] that a variety of results is expected. It does not seem likely that Jesus imagined that all His apostles would fail everywhere they went, but He also does not seem to have expected that they would all succeed. The apostles were sent out to do something that might well turn out to be impossible, in certain places and with certain people. Successful completion of the mission assigned to them by Jesus would not, necessarily, be crowned with floods of new disciples. Successful obedience to Jesus' intentions would be found in doing all that was commanded, rather than in the effort finding a positive response. In this passage, the welcome that an apostle receives is not necessarily a judgment on the ability with which he pursues his vocation or the rightness of his pursuing it.

Because we tend to read the Gospels in little bits rather than as complete wholes, we often miss the fact that they contain a sharp contrast between the overwhelming love and desire to help that Jesus exhibits toward those

---

[186] vv. 13 + 14

around Him and the very different reception He meets everywhere He goes. Even in the exchanges where Jesus seems, to Christian eyes, most clearly and obviously to be offering love and mercy to those around Him, many of those who hear Him are upset and disgusted by the things He says and does. We must realize that this hostility between Jesus and those around Him was a very real, and very constant, part of the life He lived, as it is described in the Gospels. It certainly formed Francis's own expectations of the fate that he would enjoy and the success that lay ahead for his followers.

Francis expected always to meet with difficulty both in trying to live the life he wanted to live and in trying to communicate his convictions to those around him. We know enough about his life to know that he did meet with this difficulty, over and over again. He expected to suffer practical and physical hardships, and we know that he was hungry and cold and wet and footsore and sick, for years, as he kept joyously on, suffering for the sake of his vocation.

It is clear from the lives we have to read and the stories that are told about him, that Francis recognized that the society he lived in was really not very Christian in its nature. We like to think that we live in a non-Christian society now and that earlier Christians have enjoyed an easier time than we have, but it is important for us to understand that, while the Europe St. Francis knew was nominally Christian, in reality and in detail, it was not necessarily very different from the world that Jesus knew, as far as its distance from real Christian conviction was concerned. It was really not all that different from the world that we know now.

As a matter of fact, it may well be in these same points that the life and work of Francis find their most immediate relevance for us, today. For example, we, too, should realize that living Christian lives will not be easy and will not be made easier for us by those around us. We should admit to ourselves that the society we know now, in its heart, is not very Christian. We should realize that any efforts we make to share our faith with others may very well meet with no success.

Like Francis, all of us are called to live Christian lives in a non-Christian situation. At times, probably not all the time (as is the case for some of our brethren, for example in China or the Muslim world), this will make things unpleasant for us. However, Jesus makes it clear that success is not found in the details of the life we lead or in the number of others we impress with our fervor and sanctity (if we have any fervor and sanctity to impress anyone with). After all, doing things that look religious is not really worth very much. As St. Francis, so memorably, said,[187]

> No one should flatter himself for doing anything else a sinner can also do. A sinner can...fast, pray, weep and mortify his flesh. This one thing He cannot do: be faithful to his Lord. Therefore we should glory in this: if we give back to the Lord the glory that is his, if we serve him faithfully and ascribe to him whatever he gives to us.

---

[187] Bonaventure 6.3, 58

As Francis said, anyone can **do things**, it is the faith with which we do them that matters. This truth requires two balancing acts in the life of every Christian.

First, we must work desperately hard, as Francis himself did, to dedicate ourselves with appropriate fervor to improving our Christian lives and making them the sort of lives that those around us can recognize and benefit from.

Secondly, we must make ourselves realize that nothing we do is of any ultimate value; it is, rather, the faith with which we act and the faith that makes us act that matters in our relationship with God. In fact, it is better and truer to say: it is this faith that **is** our relationship with God, at least, it is **our part** of our relationship with God. God takes care of His part of that relationship, and He is always faithful.

In the end, Francis was a saint, not because of the things he did, but because he was true to his conviction that he should do them. It is not the fact that he was cold, or hungry, or sick, or naked, or willing to look foolish in public, or willing to give up his dream to be a knight, or willing to live without a family, or willing to live without riches, or willing to live without music and dancing (which he certainly loved), that was important, it is the fact that he responded to his conviction that he should put away these things by actually setting them aside that makes him great. This is the greatness of Francis's simplicity.

Each of us, in our own way, today and going forward, can be a great saint. If we dedicate ourselves to living out our own Christian calling, we can be as true to God's will for us as Francis was to God's will for him. It may well be that none of us, even if we live up to the example of St. Francis, will live a life that looks anything like his life, from the outside. However, if we live a saintly life, it will look exactly like his life, from the inside. It will look exactly like his life from God's point of view, and that is all that matters.

Francis was a saint because he flung himself into living out his calling. If we run at our calling with that same devotion, we can be as close to God as he was. God is as ready to receive us and to meet us half-way as He was to meet Francis. All that is lacking is our willingness to do our part. All his life, Francis tried to spark that urge in those around him. Are we faithful enough to respond to that challenge?

Chapter 18

PRAYER

O Almighty God, who pourest out on all who desire it, the spirit of grace and of supplication; Deliver us, when we draw nigh to thee, from coldness of heart and wanderings of mind, that with steadfast thoughts and kindled affections, we may worship thee in spirit and in truth; through Jesus Christ our Lord. *Amen.*[188]

Francis was an ecstatic. That means that he tended to be taken outside himself (ek- out, stasis- stand, in Greek) and have what are often called "direct religious experiences". This was one of the most important elements in his make-up. His original call was to a life of prayer and solitary, devotional labor.

All through his life, he was subject to falling into ecstatic states, especially in times of prayer. This is not standard for Christians, but it is very much within the Christian Tradition. I cannot explain ecstatic prayer to you, both because I do not know how to do it and because it is said to be unexplainable. If we want to understand this part of Francis's life, we must do so second-hand. The best way for us to try to grasp Francis's experience of prayer and, so, his teachings about prayer, is to observe

---

[188] BCP, 594

them as they are reported to us by those who knew him best.

Chapter 10 of St. Bonaventure's life is a very good place for us to begin this project.[189]

He used to state firmly that the grace of prayer was to be desired above all else by a religious man, believing that without it no one could prosper in God's service. He used whatever means he could to arouse his friars to be zealous in prayer. For whether walking or sitting, inside or outside, working or resting, he was so intent on prayer that he seemed to have dedicated to it not only his heart and body but also all his effort and time. He was accustomed not to pass over negligently any visitation of the Spirit. When it was granted, he followed it, and as long as the Lord allowed, he enjoyed the sweetness offered him. When he was on a journey and felt the breathing of the divine Spirit, letting his companions go on ahead, he would stand still and render this new inspiration fruitful, not receiving the grace in vain. Many times he was lifted up in ecstatic contemplation so that, rapt out of himself and experiencing what is beyond human understanding, he was unaware of what went on around him.

---

[189] Bonaventure, 10.2, 105-106

That is a vivid description of his religious life and shows that ecstatic experiences were a recurring part of his devotions. Francis was wise enough to allow room for his ecstatic experiences and to wait upon the Holy Ghost until Its work was done and It had passed away from him. This shows that Francis recognized the truth of the Christian teaching that prayer is a conversation with God. Like any courteous person (and Francis was famous for his courtesy) Francis would not walk away or withhold his attention when God was speaking to him. He would allow the conversation to run its natural course. For Francis, as it should be for us, prayer was an open-ended thing: it allowed him to address God and God to address him, as much as He liked. This reciprocal quality is why prayer is not something that can always be done in the midst of a busy schedule without setting aside time for it: that would allow no chance for God to reply, which is, after all, the whole point of prayer, to begin with.

It is important for us to notice that, though Francis did regularly enjoy great bliss as a result of his individual prayers, he was very devoted and very scrupulous in his practice of the regular devotions that came with being a member of the Order. St. Bonaventure, who was the head of the Order (the Minister General) in his own day, is careful to point this out.[190]

> The holy man was accustomed to recite
> the canonical hours with no less reverence
> than devotion. For although he suffered from

---

[190] Bonaventure 10.6, 109. This is not the only time that Bonaventure makes this point.

an illness of the eyes, stomach, spleen and liver, nevertheless he did not want to lean against a wall while he chanted the psalms; but he said the complete hours standing erect and with head uncovered, not letting his eyes wander around and not clipping the syllables short. If he were on a journey, he would stop at the right time and never omitted this reverent and holy practice because of rain. For he used to say: "If the body requires quiet to eat its food, which along with itself will become the food of worms, with what peace and tranquility should not the soul receive the food of life?"

Like many of those who advance far in the religious life, Francis wished heartily that his prayer life could be purer and more successful. This is beautifully expressed in one of the very earliest writings about him.[191]

All his attention and affection he directed with his whole being to the one thing which he was asking the Lord, not so much praying as becoming himself a prayer.

This is a very traditional desire on the part of a Christian proficient. It has always been one of the signs of a true Christian monk to be a person of prayer. If Francis could really "become a prayer", himself, he would have managed to fulfil St. Paul's instruction that we should "pray without ceasing".[192] His life of prayer would be fully mature.

[191] Richest, 99, quoting Thomas of Celano's Second Life, sec. 95
[192] *1 Thessalonians* 5:17

The following description of Francis's practice of prayer is intended by its author to establish him as a traditional, faithful adherent to the Christian ascetical tradition. It tries to show the reader that Francis took St. Paul's teaching to heart. It is taken from the first official life the Order commissioned.[193]

> He used often to choose out solitary places in order that he might therein wholly direct his mind to God. ... For his safest haven was prayer: not prayer for one moment, not vacant or presumptuous prayer, but long-continued, full of devotion, calm and humble; if he began late he scarce ended with morning. Walking, sitting, eating, and drinking, he was intent on prayer. He would often go alone by night to pray in churches which were deserted, or in lonely places, wherein, under the protection of God's grace, he got the better of many fears and distresses of mind.

The comments about the effect that Francis's prayers had on those around him come fast and furious in all of the writings that describe him. The most famous is probably the story of the night he spent at Bernard of Quintavalle's house, a visit which was the immediate cause for Bernard becoming his first follower.[194] The story goes that Bernard invited Francis to stay with him, at a time when Francis was still being mocked and reviled by the people

---

[193] Biography, 41, from Thomas of Celano's First Life, sec. 71
[194] This story is told in the first chapter of *The Little Flowers,* which is a sign of its importance within the Franciscan tradition.

of Assisi, and Francis, after having eaten, threw himself down on the bed to sleep. Bernard, himself, pretended to go to sleep because he wanted to test Francis's sanctity. As he watched, Francis got up from the bed and prayed all night long, repeating over and over again the single phrase: "My God and my all". The effect of this on Bernard was to make him ask the next day to become Francis's first follower. The most interesting thing about that description, from our point of view, is that we notice not only the fervor of his prayer, but also the fact that it took a very simple form. Francis's devotions were never elaborate but they were always heart-felt. Great proficients in prayer only rarely seem to depend on elaborate practices to help them. It seems to be a general rule that, the more advanced a saint becomes, the less complex his practice is.

The connection between prayer and Francis's own sense of his vocation is constant and recurring in the material we have about him. For example, in the life of St. Bonaventure, at the very beginning of the second chapter, we see Francis receiving a revelation from the crucifix in the Church of St. Damian while he is at prayer.[195]

"Francis, go and repair my house, which,
as you see, is falling completely into ruin."

Bonaventure introduces prayer into his account very early and makes certain that the reader knows that Francis's famous encounter with Jesus Christ happened while he was at prayer.

If you look at art about St. Francis, you will notice (if you think of it) how often he is represented while at

---

[195] Bonaventure, 2.1, 14

prayer. (The famous fresco of Francis receiving this vision shows him kneeling before the Cross as Jesus addresses him.) We are so accustomed to seeing Francis at prayer that, if we are not careful, we will not even take conscious notice of that detail. Francis's prayers were so constant that we risk not seeing them at all. They are so omnipresent that they can become invisible.

It is interesting and important for us to notice that Francis was not a multiplier of offices or a writer of liturgies. The medieval age did produce a great amount of liturgical material, but everything we know about Francis and his idea of the Christian life shows that adding to this would have been very far from his mind. In the last chapter, when we looked at Francis's idea of poverty, we saw that story where Francis expresses the wish that the true friar would be content with only saying the Lord's Prayer.[196] While I am not certain that the story of Brother Leo's dream is really historical (it fits the purposes of the later defenders of the strict interpretation of Francis's Rule a little too well for some scholars), it makes perfect sense to think that Francis really was convinced that the Lord's Prayer was all a Christian would need. The voice that cries out:

> I would not allow anyone to become a Friar Minor unless he is content with being able to say the 'Our Father'.

sounds to me like the voice of Francis, and certainly reflects the simplicity of his own practice of prayer.

In the Sermon on the Mount, when Jesus gives His disciples instructions for their prayer, He introduces them with this phrase: "After this manner therefore pray ye"[197]

---

[196] ANF, 38-39
[197] *Matthew* 6:9

and then recites the Lord's Prayer for them. Francis's desire to take the Gospels at the most literal and simple level would naturally lead him to the conclusion that the Lord's Prayer is the only prayer necessary for the Christian to recite. (I must say that, in the abstract and on the ideal level, I think he was right. He is certainly not the only Christian saint to come to that conclusion.) However that may be, that story does tell us something important about St. Francis's idea of prayer: Francis saw prayer as a means of drawing closer to God. That means that, as long as the goal was reached, the particular prayers used were not important. Therefore, Francis would not spend time and energy trying to construct perfect liturgies. Francis was not **a writer** of prayers because he was **a prayer** of prayers. (He did not write the famous prayer that carries his name, though it is surely very "Franciscan" in its tone and content.[198]) He was so busy praying that he didn't have time to write liturgies. Francis was a practical Christian, not a theoretical one. This practicality is shown both in his fierce dedication to the practice of prayer and in his largely not bothering to put his prayers into any fancy form.

So, our brief look at Francis's practice of prayer and teaching about prayer has shown us a number of things:

Francis was one in a long line of Christians who wanted only to be close to God. Everything he did, and everything he taught, was directed toward that goal.

---

[198] Bp. Moorman, at Richest, 98-99, discusses the wording of Francis's prayers and how little we know of it. He also expresses the opinion that "The Prayer of St. Francis" is not Francis's work. That famous prayer seems to be of very recent vintage.

His approach to prayer mixed his desire for faithfulness to the Church, which we can see in his scrupulous recital of the Offices, with his desire for living a Gospel life, which is clearly expressed in his idea that only the Lord's Prayer is necessary for the Christian, or the friar, to use.

Beyond the bounds of the pattern of the Church's prayers, found in the Offices and in the Eucharist, Francis felt free to go his own way. His natural inclination was toward free-form, ecstatic prayer, and that is what he practiced.

In prayer, Francis found his greatest joy and closeness to God. Prayer, both individual and corporate, was the real heart and engine of Francis's religious life. It is important for us to say, at this point, that he was a very scrupulous and interested attender of the Eucharist and communicant at the Eucharist. Moreover, he lived in an age when this was not always the case, even for those who were seriously dedicated to Christianity, which makes his interest in Holy Communion especially noteworthy. We have already seen how much of his central conviction about the importance of humility as a part of the imitation of Christ sprang directly from his devotion to the Lord's Supper as a crowning example of Christ's humility. That should never be forgotten. Still, we should recall, also, that the many hours Francis spent in prayer, both corporate and solitary, certainly dwarfed the time he spent at celebrations of the Eucharist. In that, he was a good model of how each Christian must pray on his own in order to provide fuel for his corporate and sacramental worship life. Because of this, we should not be surprised that, in terms of the time spent and the energy expended, it was on his life of prayer that Francis found his attention most firmly fixed.

Francis was more scrupulous about his prayers than most people of his time, even most members of religious orders of whom we know. He valued the daily round of prayer because he valued the savor of God that it added to his life and because he valued the connection it offered to the whole Church, as they prayed the daily round together: separated in space but united in spirit. Francis took prayer seriously because he took his attempts to draw closer to God seriously, but he never saw the prayers as ends in themselves and always left room for God to respond or to step in and take over. In a sense, the chief lesson Francis offered through his life of prayer was that no one need re-invent the wheel when it comes to prayer. Francis followed the same steps that any could follow and said the same words that any could say. What set his prayer apart was the single-mindedness with which he engaged in it and the steadfastness of purpose with which he approached it. He showed, as clearly as anyone ever did, that prayer succeeds because of the disposition you bring to it, not because of the details of how you arrange it.

Francis took a very traditional, and a very scriptural, approach to prayer. This is true both on the level of how to practice prayer and with regard to what we should hope to gain from prayer. In the fact that he was an ecstatic, Francis was a very unusual and very advanced practicioner of Christian prayer, but in the way in which he went about it he was, actually, very much a representative of the people and a man of the Church.

Assist us mercifully, O Lord, in these our supplications and prayers, and dispose the way of thy servants towards the attainment of everlasting salvation; that, among all the changes and chances of this mortal life, they may ever be defended by thy most gracious and ready help; through Jesus Christ our Lord. *Amen.*[199]

---

[199] BCP, 49

Chapter 19

SUMMATION

O Heavenly Father, who hast filled the world with beauty; Open, we beseech thee, our eyes to behold thy gracious hand in all thy works; that rejoicing in thy whole creation, we may learn to serve thee with gladness; for the sake of him by whom all things were made, thy Son, Jesus Christ our Lord. *Amen.*[200]

We ought to spend a few pages thinking about St. Francis on a larger scale: thinking about the man as an individual and his influence in the life of the Church, during his lifetime and afterwards.

The legacy of Francis was fought over very bitterly, even during his lifetime, and the quarrel has never completely died away. We got a sense of that in some of those stories that showed the bitterness felt by the primitive Franciscans who lost the argument that took place in the Order after his death. It is evidence of how deeply Francis touches a chord in the human heart that many still feel so strongly about him, and fights that are not much less deeply felt than the ones we saw still take place in churches and at academic conferences all over the world.

I am no scholar of Francis, but I think I can safely say that, at present, all agree that the life Francis led is not the life that Franciscans lead today and that the Order he

---

[200] BCP, 596

tried to create does not exist. It may be that it never did, after those first 12 Franciscans left Rome with the pope's approval for the new Order.

It could be that Francis was trying to do an impossible thing. The mix of true humility and obedience to authority that he thought was so important may have been possible for a poor, ragged band, but it would never have been allowed in the large and growing Order. There were too many things, many of them good things, that those people could do for the Church for the hierarchy to leave them alone in their ascetical discipline. That part seems certain: I do not think the prelate has ever existed who would (or could) have left the Friars Minor alone as they expanded, with over-whelming speed, all over Latin Christendom.

It may be that the competing elements of the vocation Francis envisaged for his followers were too diverse for more than a charismatic few to juggle them successfully. To follow Francis's ideal:

- One would need to teach by action and by word
- One would need to beg for one's food
- One would need to care for the outcast
- One would need to live among the outcast
- One would need to speak boldly to the powerful
- One would need to have no settled home or planned existence.

If Francis's Order failed to materialize and the group he founded became just another western religious order (which is a good thing, I suppose, but not a new and different thing), was there any real effect of Francis's life that could not have been sparked by any founder of a religious group with an attractive character and an honest heart? Well, I think the best way to come to a conclusion on that question is to turn to the records of Francis again. Let us look at a few stories of Francis and see what thoughts they suggest to us.

Francis's trust in the Church was deep. He expected much from it and gave his Order to it without a second thought. Of course, he did this with a particular goal in mind and that goal says a great deal about what hopes he had for his Order and what he thought the Church stood in need of:[201]

> Blessed Francis said: 'I will go and entrust the Order of Friars Minor to the holy Roman Church. The rod of her authority will daunt and restrain those who wish it ill, and the sons of God will everywhere enjoy full freedom to pursue their eternal salvation. Let her sons acknowledge the kindly blessings of their Mother, and embrace her sacred feet with particular devotion.
>
> Under her protection no harm will come upon the Order, and the son of Satan will not trample over the vineyard of the Lord with impunity. Our holy Mother will herself imitate the glory of our poverty, and will not permit our observance of humility to be overshadowed by the cloud of pride. She will preserve unimpaired the bonds of love and peace that exist between us, and will impose her greatest censure on the unruly. The sacred

---

[201] Richest, 49

observance of evangelical poverty will ever
flourish before her, and she will never allow
the fragrance of our good name and holy life
to be destroyed.

In all fairness, it seems we must say that Francis's
hopes have not yet been realized. After his group fought
for almost 300 years over what it ought to be, it split in
two and each of the pieces settled into being something
much like any other religious order.[202] (They are most
like the Dominicans, I suppose, because they are focused
on education, with a heavy element of practical service,
especially for the poor and sick, too.) Any effect that the
Order has had on the Church that Francis envisaged is
not apparent, to me, at least. I do not see the transforma-
tion of the Church for which he longed and worked all
his life. Knowledge of Francis's example survives but it is
not widely followed.

If one were to argue that Francis did achieve a part
of his desire, one would hold that the witness of Francis
in the Church lives on, not so much in his Order, as in
the writings about him that the Church preserves and
still reads and that his witness still inspires Christians in
their lives and chides their weakness of commitment. I
agree. As long as these witnesses are available and known,
it cannot be said that Francis has lost the fight to have
his voice heard and his example followed in the Church.
These chapters you are reading are one of the ways that
Francis is still a living presence among Christians and the

---

[202] Bp. Moorman's History of the Franciscan Order is a standard
account of these years in the Order. (see Bibliography)

fact that it is so unsurprising for us to choose to examine Francis, in this context, for this purpose, is one of the reasons for my not being willing to say that Francis's attempt has failed and is finished.

Let me read you a rather long story from *The Mirror of Perfection*, an early source from Francis's followers, that shows us both something of how Francis read the Bible as well as how he tried to be both humble and a teacher in the Church, at the same time. I think this story shows us some of the reasons that memory of Francis endures.[203]

> ...while he was staying in Siena he was visited by a Doctor of Theology from the Order of Preachers, a man who was both humble and sincerely spiritual. When he had discussed the words of our Lord with blessed Francis for some time, this doctor asked him about the passage in Ezekiel: 'When I threaten the sinner with doom of death, it is for thee to give him word and warn him'[204]. And he said: 'Good father, I know many people who are in mortal sin, and do not warn them of their wickedness. Will their souls be required at my hand?' Blessed Francis humbly answered that he was no scholar, so that it would be more profitable for him to receive instruction from his questioner than to offer his own opinion of Scripture. The humble doctor then

---

[203] found at Richest, 55-56
[204] See *Ezekiel* 3:18-19. This is understood as the voice of God, so He is telling the prophet (and us) that those who are knowledgeable in religious matters have a duty to warn and help those who are not. (author's note)

added: 'Brother, although I have heard this passage expounded by various learned men, I would be glad to know how you interpret it'. So blessed Francis said: 'If the passage is to be understood in general terms, I take it to mean that a servant of God should burn and shine in such a way by his own life and holiness that he rebukes all wicked people by the light of his example and the devoutness of his conversation. In this way the brightness of his life and the fragrance of his reputation will make all men aware of their own wickedness'. Greatly edified, the doctor went away, and said to the companions of blessed Francis: 'My brothers, this man's theology is grounded on purity and contemplation, and resembles a flying eagle while our knowledge crawls along the ground on its belly.'

Of course, we can see in this story some signs of the tension between the followers of Francis and those of St. Dominic. Any Franciscan would be glad to hear a story that featured a Dominican Doctor of Divinity admitting that Francis was more knowledgeable than he was. There is more than that in it, however. Look at what Francis does with this quotation from *Ezekiel*. In the context of the story, the quotation is presumed to be about the religious obligation of the knowledgeable to tell the less knowing what to do. A verse like that could be used to support the growing importance of theological education in Europe and could support the place in the Church and in society of people with theological training. These people would argue that God gave them the task of telling others what to do and, so, they have an obligation to pursue it. (This requires also, of course, the connected idea that everyone else has an obligation to do what they are told by the learned since these instructions have a divine sanction.)

This could have been a terribly challenging verse for Francis, since every kind of hierarchy was counter to his vision and being in any kind of leadership role would have overturned his efforts to live out his vocation of living as the least among the least. Being a recognized teacher whom others turn to for guidance would have been as bad for Francis as being a bishop or a lord: it would have denied him his self. As a matter of fact, it is, at least, possible that the Dominican friar intentionally approached Francis with this verse in an attempt to embarrass him and to make the ideal he was propounding look foolish.

When Francis addresses this verse, however, he turns the question into an opportunity to teach a very different kind of lesson because he sees and hears everything he encounters in the context of his call to humility and his efforts to **live** a Christian life, not **talk about** or **know about** a Christian life. For Francis, everything he meets is a call to his new life of humility and penance and service, so this call to leadership becomes, in Francis's mind, a call to ever more strenuous Christian living. Instead of upsetting his sense of his vocation, this encounter strengthens it and shows the Dominican friar Francis's simplicity and the fervor of his faith.

This encounter helps us understand how Francis survived for so long with his peculiar vision intact. Francis's simplicity and singleness of purpose prevented him from being derailed on his journey. His lack of interest in being important was so complete that he could not even see a temptation in that direction when it was offered to him. The Dominican's verse might have given him a sense of his special place in the Church, but the hint fell on deaf ears. This is how human nature works. To a man who wants something for nothing, finding a wallet in the street is an easy chance for self-enrichment; to a Boy Scout eager for a merit badge, it is a heaven-sent chance to do someone a good turn: it even comes with the owner's telephone number and name! People tend to find what they are looking for because they tend to make what they find into what they want. Francis was looking for people to serve and this Dominican offered him another opportunity to do what he longed to do. He encouraged the Dominican at the same time that he gave himself more fuel to fire his own efforts. I am sure that it never occurred to him to take that verse as an opening for making a claim to dignity and power in the Church.

In the end, Francis's life and teaching came down to an attempt to proclaim two easy points:

First, the true Christian gives himself wholeheartedly to Jesus Christ. Francis declares this in the Rule he wrote for the Order in 1221:[205]

> No matter where they are, the friars must always remember that they have given themselves up completely and handed over their whole selves to our Lord Jesus Christ; and so they should be prepared to expose themselves to every enemy, visible or invisible, for love of him.

Second, the person who gives himself wholeheartedly to Jesus Christ will have Jesus' help against that part of himself that makes him stumble and struggle:[206]

---

[205] Richest, 101
[206] Richest, 102

Everyone has his own enemy in his power, and this enemy is his lower nature which leads him into sin. Blessed the religious who keeps this enemy a prisoner under his control and protects himself against it. As long as he does this, no other enemy, visible or invisible, can harm him.

That confidence did not spring from pride but from trust in God's grace. Francis dedicated his whole life to calling people to repent, but he did so because he was absolutely certain that their repentance would be answered by grace. This is, after all, what St. Paul preached, and what John the Baptist preached, and what Luther and John Wesley preached, too. This is what everyone preaches because it is the heart of what Jesus preached and made happen and endowed with power on the Cross.

Francis may have been shocking to look at and exhausting to imitate, but his message and meaning were absolutely standard Christian fare: God's love and mercy are all powerful and always being offered to any who repents honestly and asks for them. Francis's excitement never faded and his fervor never failed because they sprang from his awareness of the infinite mercy of God. The Church has never forgotten Francis because, in order to do that, she would have to forget herself and that, we are told, will never happen.[207]

Francis trusted in God's grace because he lived an ecstatic's life of communion with God. His calm certainty did not come from pride but from trust in God's mercy. All of us penitents could take heart from that message.

---

[207] *Matthew* 16:18

Paul S. Russell

Grant we beseech thee, merciful Lord, to thy faithful people pardon and peace, that they may be cleansed from all their sins and serve thee with a quiet mind; through Jesus Christ our Lord. *Amen.*[208]

---

[208] BCP, 218-219

MAKING YOUR LIFE A CHRISTIAN LIFE

Chapter 20

ORGANIZING WHAT YOU HAVE READ

The time has now come to look back at what we have seen and try to gather from these varied sources the elements in their teaching and examples that can serve us with material for our own project. What have we seen that addresses the matter of how to make our lives Christian?

We have seen that the Psalms spoke of the man who meditates on God's law and allows it to govern his behavior. He avoids the company and advice of those who do not respect God and so takes his proper place among the righteous in their congregation. Psalm 15 centered on the closeness to God that results from keeping away from the way of the wicked and holding to good behavior.

Origen's teaching on prayer can be distilled down to the idea that attention to prayer is worthwhile because of its usefulness in improving our lives rather than for its own sake.

Athanasius chimes in by putting the Psalter forward as a means of drawing near to God, conforming ourselves to Him and even drawing ourselves into a kind of union with Him by taking His words as our own and using them to think with and to address Him.

All of these really come down to the matter of paying attention to God. The core of all these teachings is a conviction that the more we cast our minds on God, the more we attend to Him in reading His Word in Scripture, the more we try to train ourselves to live our lives in parallel with His vision of virtue and justice (really, the living of human life as He has always intended it to be lived) the more we can hope to find ourselves enjoying a sense of God's presence.

Where does that leave us? So far, all of the things we have taken from the introductory background seem to be located on the "religious" level and to leave "real life" alone. Looking over the few brief paragraphs that begin this chapter has made me realize that I am in danger of falling into the trap that catches many people who are trying to focus on their religious lives: I am on the way toward thinking of our connection with God so abstractly that it may lose all contact with the life I lead when I get up in the morning. It is all very well to tell myself that "I am becoming a better person" but, if the life I lead and the things I do remain the same, how true can that claim really be? *James* 2:14-17 says it as well as it can be said, I think:

> What doth it profit, my brethren, though a man say he hath faith, and have not works? can faith save him? If a brother or sister be naked, and destitute of daily food, And one of you say unto them, Depart in peace, be ye warmed and filled; notwithstanding ye give them not those things which are needful to the body; what doth it profit? Even so faith, if it hath not works, is dead, being alone.

The words of Jesus ring in my ears, as He (and the Holy Ghost) intended them to. My own lazy (and limited) approach to the Christian life stands condemned by the Scripture and by the history of the Church.

Christians have always been people set apart from those around them by the fervor of their faith and by the zeal of their charity. Rodney Stark's interesting book, keyed on the effect of Christian charity on the growth of the Church in the Roman Empire, reinforces this conviction.[209] The fact that Christians in the ancient world thought of themselves as being defined by their new manner of life is well known among those who have studied that period, but many Christians may never have seen evidence of that for themselves. The point is so important that I think it is necessary to include the following long passage from the work of the earliest important Christian author to write in Latin, the North African lawyer, Tertullian (ca. 160-ca. 225). This passage is worth having at your disposal because it gives enough hints of the various ways its quarrelsome author thought Christians were at odds with the world around them to give us a sense of how much he thought being Christian determined the life-style of the Church's members.[210]

> We are a body knit together as such by a common religious profession, by unity of discipline, and by the bind of a common hope. We meet together as an assembly and congregation, that, offering up prayer to God as with united force, we may wrestle with Him

---

[209] See Bibliography

[210] *Apology* sec. 39, pp. 118-119 in the translation found in the Bibliography. This translation is now a part of the widely available collection *The Ante-Nicene Nicene and Post-Nicene Fathers* series reprinted by Hendricksons Publishers. That set of books is a treasure trove that every Christian should know exists.

in our supplications. This violence God delights in. We pray, too, for the emperors, for
their ministers and for all in authority, for
the welfare of the world, for the prevalence
of peace, for the delay of the final consum-
mation. We assemble to read our sacred writings, if any peculiarity of the times makes
either fore-warning or reminiscence needful.
However it be in that respect with the sacred
words, we nourish our faith, we animate our
hope, we make our confidence more stedfast;
and no less by inculcations of God's precepts
we confirm good habits. In the same place
also exhortations are made, rebukes and sacred censures are administered. For with great
gravity is the work of judging carried among
us, as befits those who feel assured that they
are in the sight of God; and you have the most
notable example of judgment to come when
any one has sinned so grievously as to require
his severance from us in prayer, and the meeting, and all sacred intercourse. The tried men
of our elders preside over us, obtaining that
honour not by purchase, but by established
character. There is no buying and selling of
any sort in the things of God. Though we
have our treasure-chest, it is not made up of
purchase-money, as of a religion that has its
price. On the monthly collection day, if he
likes, each puts in a small donation; but only
if it be his pleasure, and only if he be able: for
there is no compulsion; all is voluntary. These
gifts are, as it were, piety's deposit fund. For

they are not taken thence and spent on feasts,
and drinking-bouts, and eating-houses, but
to support and bury poor people, to supply
the wants of boys and girls destitute of means
and parents, and of old persons confined now
to the house; such, too, as have suffered ship-
wreck; and if there happen to be any in the
mines, or banished to the islands, or shut up
in the prisons, for nothing but their fidelity
to the cause of God's church, they become
the nurslings of their confession. But it is
mainly the deeds of a love so noble that lead
many to put a brand upon us. See, they say,
how they love one another…"

I might feel the need to apologize for deluging you
with such a flood of early Christian eloquence except that
I know that every teacher can only pass on the things
he knows. My training is in the history of Christian
Thought, especially the early period, so I offer you some
of the things I know. If you are encouraged to look backward into the Christian past for guidance and encouragement I will be very glad, no matter what period of the
Church's life speaks to you most powerfully.

The Holy Ghost (through St. James), Tertullian and
I are all trying to tell you the same thing: fully developed
Christianity can only be found in those who not only
direct their minds and hearts toward God, but who also
direct their lives toward Him.

Our two central subjects of study: the Desert Fathers of Egypt and St. Francis of Assisi might, at the first
glance, have seemed to be flying off in a very different
direction from this concern for others. Their fervor was

so overwhelming and their lives were so exotic that I have heard both of them called "selfish" by modern people who knew only enough about them to know their reputations. How inadequate that judgment should seem, to us, after we have studied them up-close!

The whole project of creating the Desert literature, as well as the teaching and visiting that it records, is clear evidence of a desire to help their fellow believers. The stories of the entertaining of visitors by the monks show that their charitable concern reached beyond the group of those who sought to live as they did to all Christians who yearned for help and comfort and came (or sent others) to them in hopes that they could guide them.

St. Francis, far from being wholly wrapped up in his own concerns, spent much of his time and most of his energy trying to guide his growing Order and trying to explain it, and himself, to those who sought him out. From the sultan in Egypt to the peasants in the fields he walked past on his journeys, Francis engaged all he met with open honesty and good will. He was ready to give the Bible out of his chapel to the poor and willing to throw himself into the fire to spark a conversion in the Sultan.[211] The fact that we do not know which of those things was harder for him to do shows how clear our own idea of his hopes is and how uncertain, on the other hard, is the record of his personal desires.

When we look at all our sources squarely, then, we see that the Christian tradition is telling us that **all** of ourselves, **all** of our lives (both the interior and the exterior) must be focused on drawing close to God and on forming ourselves to Him. Thus, in turning from our

---

[211] Bonaventure 9.8, 270

background section to the central examples of our volume, we drew the Christian teaching into clearer and more detailed focus, but what we found was another version of the same picture.

So, we see that the teaching of the Desert Fathers runs along very much the same lines as the Psalms and our two early Egyptians. Their emphases on fasting and on practical charity are both supports of this same desire for attention to God. In their experience, fasting helps the Christian because of the training of the will that it involves, which makes it easier for us to apply that will to attending to God when we are at worship or at study. Practical charity is an aid precisely because it fulfills the central commandment of loving our neighbor as ourselves and, so, helps mold us into better images of God. It also, of course, helps to fill our lives with good activities and thoughts and so gives the activities and thoughts that might lead us astray less room to trouble us. (There is much hard-won wisdom in that realization of the value of pursuing the good.)

St. Francis, too, shows all those same qualities:
- He makes much use of fasting to focus his heart and mind.
- He is fervent in his pursuit of chances to practice charity.
- He spends large parts of his time at prayer, trying to draw himself into the presence of God.

These practices all seem to be directed at this same goal of learning how to attend to God more effectively and to pursue His presence more conscientiously.

So, at the conclusion of our historical study, we can gather the teachings and practices we have collected into a few broad categories of things that we can do to try to make our lives Christian ones:

We can try to train our wills through the practice of ordering our lives on special lines. (This can be both positive and negative; it can involve either adding things in or taking things out.)

We can try to attend to God more closely through the reading of the Bible or through prayer. (Of course, we can also try a mixture of both, which would be the best solution. It would allow us to gain both sorts of benefits while also engaging our minds and imaginations to their fullest capacity.)

We can try to act in ways that agree with God's will, the first and most important way being the practice of love of neighbor.

Those ideas are all clear, even obvious, to any Christian. The trick will lie in how to apply them in the real world. We turn to that in our final chapter.

Chapter 21

BEGINNING TO LIVE THE CHRISTIAN LIFE

Now that we have re-acquainted ourselves with what our sources offer in terms of teaching on how to construct a Christian life (or, to put it more exactly and more attractively, how to further the work of God's grace in us so that we may become what He is working to make us be), the time has come to move from preparation and reflection to action. What are we to do?

It is 2,000 years, almost, since the public ministry of Jesus began and people first set themselves to the task of trying to live as His disciples. During that whole period, Christians have been busy writing things to help each other in their attempts to follow Jesus. Already at the time of writing the concluding chapter of *The Gospel according to St. John* the evangelist was overwhelmed at the prospect of all the books that Christians could write, and his fears were not misplaced.[212] While it may disappoint those of you who hope to have your ears scratched with something new[213], you ought to be relieved that the concluding chapter of this book is so brief and claims to offer nothing extraordinary.

---

[212] *John* 21:25: "And there are also many other things which Jesus did, the which, if they should be written every one, I suppose that even the world itself could not contain the books that should be written."

[213] See *2 Timothy* 4:3

The main force of the teaching that this book contains is in the examples set out and the stories of earlier Christians engaged in the same struggle we know. You would not benefit from hearing me say more flatly what these great saints have shown in their own lives and taught by their words. What remains for us to do is to live up to their example by an earnest effort at walking in their steps. All this chapter can possibly do is to offer a few concrete suggestions about how to begin. Once you have started on your own discipleship, you will quickly move beyond the bounds of where I can be of help to you. At that point, and forever after, you must allow the Holy Ghost, the Bible and the Church to guide you. We are fortunate in having the Church, that "so great a cloud of witnesses"[214], with us to whom we can turn and on whom we can depend for guidance toward God. The fact that we can all be each others' guides while also being pilgrims on the way is one of the surest signs of the active grace of God in the world that I know. So, now we turn to the task.

As with all attempts to improve the things we do and the lives we lead, it is the ability to stick with the resolutions we make and to allow the new activities and attitudes we are trying to cultivate to blossom into their full form that will separate a successful effort to begin christianizing our lives from one that fails. In a culture in which virtually all members have access to too much of the world's goods (where in history do we see another society whose poor suffered from obesity as ours do?) dieting may be the most easily understood example to use

---

[214] *Hebrews* 12:1

when we settle down to consider the concrete things we ought to do to set out on the Christian path. Those who try extravagant and exhausting diets almost always follow them for only a short time, while those who can stick to their resolutions, even if they are much more modest, are much more likely to succeed in the end. Spritual discipline and dieting are both areas in which the race goes to the tortoise rather than the hare.

The fact that the first known name for Christianity, one that appears a number of times in the New Testament, was "the Way"[215] is a clear indication of the fact that the very earliest Christians thought of their new faith as a process that was dynamic and progressive rather than a state that was unchanging. "Christian" is not really a status that one attains and then stays there; it is, instead, something one is always striving to become. No one who expects his efforts to bring quick results can possibly succeed at the long, patient process necessary for real progress in the Christian Faith. So, the first element that we must cultivate is **patience**.

What, then, is the first step? For each of us this will be different because each of us must examine the life he leads and the responsibilities he has before he begins to rearrange them. It is an important Christian principle, taught most vividly by Christ in the Parable of the Good Samaritan, that no one should push aside his responsibility toward others in pursuit of fulfilling religious duties. No mother of small children should take on a rule of prayer and Scripture reading that interferes with her care for her family. No father supporting a family should structure his time so as to make his job suffer and the

---

[215] *Acts* 9:2, 19:9 + 23, 22:4, 24:22 are all examples of this.

family's livelihood to be put in jeopardy. No child in school should cast aside his schoolwork to read the Bible and find himself failing at the practical task his stage of life demands. Our search for a more fully Christian life is not, in the first instance, an occasion to step completely out of the life we already are living. Instead, it is a chance to find a way to infuse that life with Christian purpose and allow it (and us) to show our religious identity to the world by how we live.[216] So, how can we discover what parts of our lives we can change and what parts we cannot? What are the boundaries that must guide the choices we make as we try to reorganize how we spend our time? How do we decide what our lives allow us to do?

We must separate the things we do into distinct categories: those that are necessary for what we are trying to accomplish in life, those that are helpful for these purposes and those that are purely voluntary or pursued only for enjoyment's sake. All that is necessary must, by its nature, continue to be performed. Food must be bought, jobs must be performed, babies must be bathed and dressed, etc. It is crucially important to realize, however, that it is a mistake to think that these are immovable obstacles that serve only to inhibit the things we really want to do.

---

[216] There are, of course, circumstances in which Christian faith does demand a complete change, no one would deny that. If you are an interrogator of prisoners for the North Korean government and you become a Christian, you are not called to "torture your prisoners more fully and with greater conviction and offer that work to Jesus". It would be blasphemy to suggest such a thing. This sort of example has little direct application to the lives of most modern western people, thank goodness. Our lives are not lived in an atmosphere of such degradation and squalor. Our troubles are of another sort.

These are all religious duties in themselves, if they are properly understood, and many of them are among the greatest joys this world can offer. What could offer more real pleasure than a walk on a lovely day with a baby in a stroller? It should be performed for the child's health and welfare, but few parents would think it is a burden. (Indeed, having no child younger than 11 is a very bittersweet thing for me.) I could go on and on about these tasks: who would want to live in a house without any food at hand or never wash clothing or linens or never bathe? God has so constituted our natures that many of the things that are necessary for our health and tranquility are also enjoyable. We should be glad that this is so. This group of activities is not made up of irksome burdens but of necessary tasks: caring for the aged and the young, keeping up a house so that the roof and pipes do not leak, making sure that our car starts if needed. It is the fact that sufficient time and effort is due to these things and must be set aside that makes us begin here. The other categories must be made to fit around these since they are immovable.

The remaining parts of our lives, the helpful and the voluntary, are those that offer us some scope for action and planning. It helps to clear the first category to the side but we still must give some thought to what remains. Practical questions come first when determining the possible choices we may have.

- When during the day are our helpful and voluntary activities found?
- When during the week are they found? (Are they all bunched on just a few days or are they spread out over the entire week?)

- How dependable is the schedule according to which our life is structured?

Devotion

If you normally spend two hours in the morning reading the newspaper and watching morning television, then, unless you are a media critic for whom this is research necessary to your work, you have a large chunk of the day that you can apply to the task of Christianizing your life, if you are willing. Morning hours are especially valuable because you are likely to be more alert and more able to apply yourself efficiently to the task, then, than you would be at the day's end. It is not surprising that Christians have traditionally sought ways to begin the day with prayer and Bible study. Our minds are fresh, other people may well not yet be awake or be busy with other things and there is often enough time before the work day begins for its approach not to impinge on our consciousness.

Half an hour of attentive prayer followed by Bible reading (15 minutes of each is a good amount to start with) is a great boost to focusing your mind and heart on God for the rest of the day. If you have a longer amount of time to spend on voluntary activities than you intend to spend on devotion, **always do your devotion first**. Then your helpful and voluntary activities can be fully enjoyed because you have cleared the way for them. If you really want to spend time on devotion and have not done it yet, that lack will lodge in the back of your mind and will interfere with your amusements. Getting your devotion under your belt is not only a way of starting your day with God, it is also a way to make sure that you do not need to worry that your enjoyment of the things you do for fun will keep you at them for so long that your devotion is squeezed to the point of disappearing.

If you have duties that arise immediately when you wake up in the morning (in my experience, these have almost always involved caring for children, though this has changed from diapers and feeding to feeding and carpool, over the years) then you must put your devotions off to a later time. Reminding yourself as you work that what you do is not only something you want to do but also the fulfillment of God's commandment that we should care for our neighbors (family are our nearest neighbors) may seem a self-congratulatory thing to do, but I think it is a plain fact.

In Chapter 10 we saw that long story of the learned priest who asked to join Francis's followers and was first put off and then, only grudgingly, allowed to work in the kitchen. What should he have done during that month before he was recalled (a time that, for all he knew, might have lasted until the end of his life) except tell himself that this kitchen service was his religious duty and he was fortunate to know what his duty was and to be able to perform it? Is that a more saintly thought than for a parent to think the same thing while making breakfast or packing lunches? I have known many people who downgrade the performance of routine domestic duties of this sort but I think they are blind to the reality before their eyes. Some of that is our mercantile society's instinct to scorn anything that is not well paid. (Ask a teacher if he or she feels greatly respected!) Some of it, though, is just the effect of the overwhelming sameness of these duties, day in and day out. The 400th plate of macaroni and cheese one produces is not much more skillfully done than the first and one has little sense of the grandeur of life while boiling the noodles. We all feel the dullness of routine, but that, you will quickly find, is present just as much in prayer and Bible reading as it is in making peanut butter and jelly sandwiches on white bread.

We like to think that the things we do are particularly difficult and particularly onerous. Part of this conviction comes from the fact that our own tedium (like our own pain) is much more real to us than that of other people, but some of it, I think, comes from our silent conviction of our own uniqueness. It may be a helpful thing to hear a word of teaching of the desert father Agathon when he was asked about the varying difficulty of different deeds.[217]

> The brethren also asked him, 'Amongst all good works, which is the virtue which requires the greatest effort? He answered, 'Forgive me, but I think there is no labour greater than that of prayer to God. For every time a man wants to pray, his enemies, the demons, want to prevent him, for they know that it is only by turning him from prayer that they can hinder his journey. Whatever good work a man undertakes, if he perseveres in it, he will attain rest. But prayer is warfare to the last breath.'

One of Abba Agathon's points is that the religious value of prayer, the closeness to God and advancement in virtue it can bring, makes it more difficult for us. All the

---

[217] #9, 21 in Ward Alphabetical

spiritual forces in the world that work to draw us away from God work especially hard when we are engaged in something as good as prayer. This insight is important for our view of life's practicalities, too.

If care of our neighbor is one of our primary religious duties and that care, at the present, is expressed in care of our children, then the unglamorous drudgery of carpool trips and supervising homework is just where the demons will strike, in Abba Agathon's picture. The purer is the religious duty, the stronger the temptations to shirk or scorn it. He does hold out hope that the spiritually advanced can win through to the end in the realm of practical charity (so there is hope for mothers, after all) but "Prayer is warfare to the last breath" in his experience. Why?

It may be that our human nature, part physical and part spiritual, can draw strength and sustenance from a feeling of accomplishment at our good deeds, as deeds. The gratitude of those we help, the neatness of a carefully swept floor, the satisfaction of a wall well built, may speak to a deep part of us. Prayer, of all things the least substantial (but, spiritually, the purest and most central) may not offer us that nourishment. Or, it may be nothing more exotic than the fact that every little old lady he helps across the street is in some way unique to the Boy Scout who helps her, but every time we say the Lord's Prayer it is exactly the same. The prospect of making 365 peanut butter and jelly sandwiches per year for the next five years might daunt the fondest parent, but how much more daunting is the ideas of reciting the Lord's Prayer 730 times each year, plus 52 Sundays, plus any other religious services, every year for the rest of your life? The prospect stretches out before us of an unending sequence of repetition. No wonder it is "warfare to the last breath"! The only thing that can take away the feeling of being swamped in religious obligations is the picture of weaving prayer into one's life like a special thread in a cloth and the reflection that we only need face one day at a time. In prayer, as in all these central aspects of life, trying to face it all at once is too much, but taking it as it comes is manageable, and even comforting. At least, it is for me. A bit of true perspective on this point can be a great encouragement.

The next obvious opportunity for a change of routine is in the middle of the day. Virtually everyone has a time set aside for a mid-day meal. (If you work in food service, then this will come unusually early or unusually late in the day, but it will still be present at some point.) At this point, things begin to become much more individualized.

If this is your first real moment to breathe during the day then you might like to do what others have done earlier and try to pair prayer and Scripture. However, if your workplace makes it difficult for you to have a Bible at hand or to have brought one with you to work at all or if you have no place to go to read it, then you should content yourself with prayer. If circumstances demand, you may need to say these silently to yourself while eating or doing something else.

Some Christians in America feel greatly put upon if they cannot order their devotions exactly as they see fit in a manner that they find comfortable and welcoming. This attitude is so out of touch with the predicament in which so many millions of our brothers and sisters have lived out their lives (and that so many now experience) that it is hard to listen to complaints of this kind with even the semblance of charity. A moment's reflection on how little difficulty we must undergo to perform our worship [and an extra prayer for Christians who live in lands of persecution (all of the Muslim world, just as a start)] should help us past that feeling of being ill-used. As a matter of fact, the experience of needing to adjust our devotional practices to fit the practicalities of our lives is actually good for us, in at least two ways.

First, it reminds us of what we are trying to do: make the life we are **already living** a Christian life. That is, we are trying to alter the character of something that already exists rather than beginning from scratch to build a pattern of life that meets all our abstract ideas of what would be "best". As a matter of fact, what is "best" is what works best for us in our particular time and place. What is "best" will, most likely, change a number of times as we go along through life. One of the benefits of being made to fit our religious practice into a schedule that is not designed with it in mind is that it makes us aware that our current arrangement is always contingent and fitted to the situation. It makes us keep our eyes open for a chance to change our religious practice for the better.

Second, it makes us aware of the great blessing we enjoy in living in a culture that is more ignorant of the Gospel than it is hostile to it. This means that we do not really need to be afraid of persecution in the way many of our brothers and sisters do. It also means that we may hope that our style of life and religious devotions may be noticed by those around us and cause them to want to learn more. Do not think that I am suggesting that we make any parade of our religion or that we announce to those around us what we are doing. I am not doing any such thing and I am very much aware of Our Lord's instructions that we should avoid any kind of show-off religiosity.[218] However, I do know that occasions arise when people ask about Christianity and that these are often sparked by their noticing something different about what we do or say. (Tertullian was right, in that regard.) If an occasion of this sort does confront you, it will be because of the mixed world we live in and may be the intention of the Holy Ghost that is at work. It is certainly a case of God making all things work together for good.[219] Our inconvenience may become someone else's call to faith.

The close of the day may offer another chance for devotion, this time will be less efficient, and Bible study will be less fruitful, because both mind and body are weary, but an evening 20 minutes of prayer and Scripture can sanctify the day's end and prepare you for the night's rest.

Traveling Time

Americans in our age spend a lot of time getting places. We drive to work and school and play. We get in each other's way when we travel and slow each other down. We sit in our cars, listening to the radio and going nowhere. All of this is a great trial, but it is also an opportunity that we can turn to better uses. This is where the suggestions I first made in Chapter 3 would come in handy.

---

[218] See *Matthew* 6:1-6 for a famous example. I do not think I need to argue this point. We all are aware of the dangers of self-satisfaction in religion, I hope.
[219] *Romans* 8:28

The Desert Fathers, who worked to support themselves, spent most of their time praying and reciting Psalms while doing something else with their hands. Most commonly, they spent their days weaving baskets from palm fronds (a marginal skill at best in North America, though I have seen it being done) which was well suited to using one's mind for a different task. That is probably not something that we will all take up, but their practice of leavening their work with prayer and devotion is something that can be very useful.

I suggest that you set yourself the task of committing to memory several shorter Psalms and some prayers beyond the Lord's Prayer. (Because I am an Anglican, *The Book of Common Prayer* is the obvious place for me to turn for this, and I commend it to you if you do not know it[220], but there are other sources that will supply what you need.) Once you have found suitable raw material and have it in your head, you can begin to recite it as you drive or sit on the bus or walk. (I have found walking and jogging particularly conducive to recitation and prayer. The colonnades that surround the courtyards of so many monasteries in the West bear witness to this fact. They were built with the intention that they would serve to shelter people in their slow, meditative walking during prayer and Bible reading. Try it sometime; you may be surprised how helpful it can be.) Long practice has taught Christians that, after you do this for some time, you will find these Psalms and prayers playing themselves over and over again in the back of your mind the way popular songs can do (especially if you don't really care

---

[220] See Bibliography

Paul S. Russell

for them). This is one way of working yourself toward St. Paul's goal of praying without ceasing.

When You Have No Time

There are times in life when we have so much to do that we really have no time for the non-essentials. (There are more people around who *say* they have "no time" than there are who *really* have no time, but the problem can exist.) It would be very unusual for it to be the common state of one's life but most of us have periods of intense activity and unrest, now and again. What are we to do with these?

The savvy Christian who is going through one of these patches in his life can do only 4 things:

- Tell yourself that this is not a permanent state
- Apply yourself diligently to the things that you must do
- Make use of your memorized prayers and Psalms as often as you can
- Remind yourself that the things that make you so busy are part of your duty to God.

If you are running yourself ragged at work, you are supporting yourself and your family, which you must do. If you are running ragged because of family responsibilities, sickness, death, an approaching wedding or something else out of the ordinary, then you are caring for your neighbors. (If you are being run down for something other than home or family or work then you need to consider seriously if this is something that you should be involved with.)

Moving Forward

In principle and, I believe, in fact, any stage of your life should be open to being leavened with a more conscious Christian cast and a more consciously Christian understanding of its value and purpose. As you spend more time trying to import the awareness of God into your life every day, experience teaches that the way you think of the things you do and even the way you do them will change. Christians report that this experience will build on and support itself if we persist in it and that we will discover that it becomes (in the main) easier to do and more successful as time goes on.

We must always be ready for failure, while doing our best to avoid it, and we must always expect that the struggle will be a part of our lives. This struggle is not a sign of failure, it is merely the evidence of our living as fallen humans in a fallen world.

So, we end with the very thought that lay behind the need for us to begin: the fact that we live our lives more or less estranged from God in a world that is more or less estranged from Him, too. If our predicament were not what it is, we would not need to pour our attention into drawing closer to God for He would be present to our consciousness all the time. The difficulties we know are symptoms of the problem we are trying to solve. We should not expect anything else.

GENERAL BIBLIOGRAPHY

(The words in parentheses after each entry in all three
sections denote how it is referred to in the notes.)

Aphrahat, *Demonstrations* I
Translated from Syriac and introduced by Kuriakose Va-
lavanolickal
HIRS Publications Mar Thoma Vidyanikethan Changa-
nassery, Kerala (India) 1999
(Aphrahat, *Demonstrations* I)

Aphrahat the Persian Sage, *Selections Translated into English from the Demonstrations*, John Gwynn
The Nicene and Post-Nicene Fathers (sec. ser.) volume 13,
pp. 345-412
Grand Rapids. Mich.: Eerdmans Publishing 1989 (reprint)
(Aphrahat, *Selections*)

*Athanasius The Life of Antony and The Letter to Marcel-
linus* Translation and Introduction by Robert C. Gregg
New York, NY: Paulist Press 1980
(Gregg, *Athanasius*)

*The Book of Common Prayer and Administration of the
Sacraments and Other Rites and Ceremonies of the Church
according to the use of the Protestant Episcopal Church in
the United States of America Together with the Psalms of
David*
The Seabury Press, New York 1928
(BCP)

Sebastian Brock, "Early Syrian Asceticism"
Numen XX (1977)
Reprinted as I in *Syriac Perspectives on Late Antiquity*
Aldershot, Hampshire: Ashgate Publishing 1997
(Brock, Asceticism)

Peter Brown, *Society and the Holy in Late Antiquity*
Berkeley, CA: University of California Press 1982

A.S.T. Fisher, *An Anthology of Prayers Compiled for use in School and Home*
London: Longmans, Green and Co. 1935 (2nd ed.)
(Fisher)

Ian Gillman and Hans-Joachim Klimkeit, *Christians in Asia before 1500*
Ann Arbor: The University of Michigan Press 1999
(Gilman and Klimkeit)

Sidney H. Griffith, "Asceticism in the Church of Syria: The Hermeneutics of Early Syrian Monasticism", 220-45 in Vincent L. Wimbush and Richard Valantasis (ed.), *Asceticism*
Oxford University Press 1995
(Griffith, Asceticism)

Sidney H. Griffith, "'Singles' in God's Service; Thoughts on the Ihidaye from the Works of Aphrahat and Ephraem the Syrian", 145-159 in
The Harp 4, 1-3 (July 1991)
(Griffith, Singles)

Susan Ashbrook Harvey, "The Edessan Martyrs and Ascetic Tradition"
The Harp, 6.2 (November 1993), 99-110
(Harvey)

The New Jerome Biblical Commentary
(ed.) Raymond E. Brown, S.S., Joseph A. Fitzmyer, S.J., Roland E. Murphy, O.Carm.
Prentice Hall 1990

C.S. Lewis, *Reflections on the Psalms*
New York: Harcourt Brace & Company 1958

Tremper Longman III, *How to Read the Psalms*
Downers Grove, Ill.: InterVarsity Press 1988

Samuel Hugh Moffett, *A History of Christianity in Asia*
(2 vols.)
Maryknoll, NY: Orbis Books 1998/2005
(Moffett)

George Nedungatt, S.J., "The Covenanters of the Early Syriac-Speaking Church"
Orientalia Christiana Periodica 39 (1973) 191-215 and 419-444
(Nedungatt)

Origen An Exhortation to Martyrdom, Prayer and Selected Works, Translation and Introduction by Rowan A. Greer
New York, NY: Paulist Press 1979
(Greer, Origen)

James Oulton and Henry Chadwick, *Alexandrian Christianity*
Philadelphia: The Westminster Press 1954
(Oulton and Chadwick)

The Oxford Dictionary of the Christian Church (rev. sec. ed.)
Edited by F.L. Cross and E.A. Livingstone
Oxford University Press 1983
(ODCC)

Paul S. Russell, "Syriac Christianity: Yesterday, Today and Forever"
The Journal of Maronite Studies 5, 1 (January-April 2001)
www.mari.org
(Russell)

Nahum M. Sarna, *On the Book of Psalms* Exploring the Prayers of Ancient Israel
New York: Schocken Books 1993

Rodney Stark, *The Rise of Christianity: How the Obscure, Marginal Jesus Movement Became the Dominant Religious Force in the Western World in a Few Centuries*
San Francisco: HarperSanFrancisco 1997

Tertullian, *The Apology*, 53-140 in Volume XI of
Ante-Nicene Christian Library Translations of the Writings of the Fathers Down to A.D. 325, edited by the Rev. Alexander Roberts, D.D. and James Donaldson, L.L.D.
Edinburgh: T. & T. Clark 1869
(Tertullian)

BIBLIOGRAPHY FOR CHAPTERS ON FRANCIS OF ASSISI

Regis J. Armstrong, *Francis of Assisi, Early Documents:*
Vol. 1, The Saint;
Vol. 2, The Founder; Vol. 3, The Prophet
New City Press 2002
(These three volumes make up the most recent and most complete collection of material.)

Regis J. Armstrong and Ignatius C. Brady, *Francis and Clare: The Complete Works*
(The Classics of Western Spirituality)
Mahwah, NJ: Paulist Press 1986

Joseph Bingham, *Origines Ecclesiasticae; or, the Antiquities of the The Christian Church, and other works of the Rev. Joseph Bingham, M.A.* (9 volumes)
London: William Straker 1843
(Bingham)

Bonaventure, *The Life of St. Francis*
Harper Collins Spiritual Classics
HarperSanFrancisco 2005
(Bonaventure)

Raphael Brown, *The Little Flowers of St. Francis*
Garden City, NY: Image Books 1958
(This work exists in many editions. This is one of the most widely read spiritual books in western Christianity. It requires more background knowledge than most readers possess.)

(The Little Flowers)

G.K. Chesterton, *St. Francis of Assisi*
George H. Doran Company 1928 (much reprinted, now by Ignatius Press)
(A thrilling read, but not to be depended on for reliable information.)

Omer Englebert, *St. Francis of Assisi A Biography*
Cincinnati, Ohio: St. Anthony Messenger Press 1979 (reissue)
(This is an interesting combination of a saint's life and a modern biography.)
(Englebert)

Marion A. Habig (ed.), *St. Francis of Assisi: Writings and Early Biographies: English Omnibus of the Sources for the Life of St. Francis*
Franciscan Herald Press 1996 (4th revised edition)
[also available from Quincy, Ill.: Franciscan Press Quincy University 1991 (2 vols.)]
(This was the English standard before Armstrong's trilogy.)
(Habig)

John R.H. Moorman, *A History of the Franciscan Order from Its Origins to the Year 1517*
Oxford University Press 1968
Chicago: Franciscan Herald Press 1988
(History)

John R.H. Moorman, D.D., *A New Fioretti* A Collection of Early Stories about Saint Francis of Assisi hitherto untranslated

London: SPCK 1946
(very interesting tales with short introductions)
(ANF)

John R.H. Moorman, *Richest of Poor Men* The Spirituality of St. Francis of Assisi
London: Darton, Longman & Todd 1977
(Richest)

John R.H. Moorman, *St. Francis of Assisi*
London: SCM Press 1950
Chicago, Ill.: Franciscan Herald Press 1976 (reprint)
(This is a very intelligent account; a good place to start, but hard to find.)
(Biography)

L.V. Rutgers, P.W. van der Horst, H.W. Havelaar, L. Teugels (eds.), *The Use of Sacred Books in the Ancient World*
Louvain: Peeters Press 1998
(Rutgers)

BIBILIOGRAPHY AND A SELECTION OF BOOKS ON THE DESERT AND THE DESERT ASCETICS

The Letters of Ammonas, translated by Derwas J. Chitty
Oxford: SLG Press 1979

The Letters of Saint Antony the Great, translated by Derwas J. Chitty
Oxford: SLG Press 1975

Letters from the Desert, Barsanuphius and John
Crestwood, NY: Saint Vladimir's Seminary Press 2003

Seeking a Purer Christian Life The Desert Fathers and Mothers, arranged, edited and introduced by Keith Beasley-Topliffe
Nashville: Upper Room Books 2000

The Word in the Desert Scripture and the Quest for Holiness in Early Christian Monasticism, Douglas Burton-Christie
Oxford University Press 1993

Selected Writings of St. John Cassian the Roman
Stafford, AZ: St. Paisius Orthodox Women's Monastery 2000

The Desert a City, Derwas J. Chitty
Crestwood, NY: St. Vladimir's Seminary Press 1966

*Four Desert Fathers Pambo, Evagrius, Macarius of Egypt &
Macarius of Alexandria* Coptic Texts relating to the *Lau-
siac History* of Palladius, translated by Tom Vivian
Crestwood, NY: Saint Vladimir's Seminary Press 2004

Journey Back to Eden My Life and Times Among the Desert Fathers, Mark Gruber, OSB
Maryknoll, NY: Orbis Books 2002

William Harmless, *Desert Christians: An Introduction to
the Literature of Early Monasticism*
Oxford University Press 2004

David Knowles, *Christian Monasticism*
New York, NY: McGraw-Hill Book Company 1969

St. Macarius the Spiritbearer Coptic Texts relating to Saint
Macarius the Great, translated by Tom Vivian
Crestwood, NY: Saint Vladimir's Seminary Press 2004

The Wisdom of the Desert, Thomas Merton
The Abbey of Gethsemani, Inc. 1960

The Spiritual Meadow of John Moschus, translated by John
Wortley
Kalamazoo, Michigan: Cistercian Publications 1992

The Desert An Anthology for Lent, John Moses
Harrisburg, PA: Morehouse Publishing 1997

The Life and Teaching of Pachomius
Leominster, Herefordshire: Gracewing 1998

The Day-to-Day Life of the Desert Fathers in Fourth Century Egypt, Lucien Regnault
Petersham, Mass.: St. Bede's Publications 1999

The Lives of the Desert Fathers, Norman Russell
Kalamazoo, Mich: Cistercian Publications 1980

The World of the Desert Fathers, Columba Stewart, OSB
Kalamazoo, Mich: Cistercian Publications 1986

The Desert Fathers, Helen Waddell
Vintage 1998 (reprint)
(Waddell)

The Desert Fathers Sayings of the Early Christian Monks,
Benedicta Ward
Penguin Books 2003
(Ward Penguin)

The Sayings of the Desert Fathers The Alphabetical Collection, Benedicta Ward, SLG
Oxford: Mowbray & Co. Ltd. 1981 (revised edition)
(Ward Alphabetical)

The Wisdom of the Desert Fathers, compiled by Benedicta Ward
Oxford: Lion Publishing 1998
(Ward Wisdom)

The Wisdom of the Desert Fathers, Benedicta Ward, SLG
Oxford: Fairacres Publications 1986 (new ed.)

LaVergne, TN USA
04 April 2011
222767LV00001B/59/P

9 781438 923383